YAYOI KUSAMA

A Dream I Dreamed

目錄

CONTENTS

給台灣的話

台灣，似近似遠，是我的愛的故鄉。對台灣在國際社會上的艱難與愛的願望，我始終帶著最大的關心與敬意。
願以我人生大量的愛，獻上我奮鬥至今的所有藝術。獻給對人類生命的讚嘆、廣大天空的白雲壯志、這片土地上美麗生物的生存樣態、美麗的蔚藍大海，以及眾人愛的嘆息，還有始終憧憬生命的你們。
衷心希望大家能看到我的愛的藝術，在台灣的天空及靄靄白雲下平靜地綻放光芒。

我殷切期盼大家能珍愛自己的生命，正視人類在生命盡頭最大的願望。

我所愛的台灣朋友們，讓我們一起分享人生吧。
在任何艱難的時刻中，也要朝自己的願望邁進！

獻給愛之所在，台灣的朋友們。

草間彌生

台湾へのメッセージ

台湾は、近くて遠くにある私の愛の故郷でもありました。そして私は国際社会の中におかれた、台湾の苦労と愛の願望に対して、多大の関心と敬意を抱いてきました。

人間に対する命への賛美と広大な空の白い雲の志、地上の美しい生物の生き様、美しい青い海、そして多くの方々の愛のため息と生命へのあこがれを持って生きてこられたあなたたちに、私は多大の人生の愛をもって、私の闘ってきたすべての芸術を捧げたいと思います。

皆さんが、台湾の空や白い雲の下に穏やかに光る、私の愛の芸術を見出してくださることを切望しています。

自らの生命を愛し、生命の果ての人類の最大の願望を見つめていくこと、それが私の切なる願いです。

わが愛する台湾の人々、共に人生を分かち合ってまいりましょう。
どんな大変なことがあっても、自分たちの願いを立ち上げることを!

愛の住処、台湾の人々へ。

草間弥生

Words for Taiwan

Taiwan, so near and yet so far, is my beloved homeland. I have always had the greatest concern and respect for Taiwan, which has faced such difficulties in international society but still wishes for love.

I have sought to contribute all the love I have ever felt for the art that I have struggled to create throughout my life. I also wish to contribute the admiration I have for human life, the majesty of the white clouds in the vast sky, the survival of all the beautiful living things in this land, the lovely azure sea, everyone's sighs of love, and your ceaseless longing for life.

I sincerely hope that everyone will see my art, which is dedicated to love, serenely glitering under Taiwan's sky and billowing white clouds.

I earnestly hope that everyone will cherish his/her own life and look squarely at people's greatest wish when they are reaching the end of life.

My beloved friends in Taiwan, let us share life together.
At all difficult moments, let us continue to strive for our own aspirations!

To my friends in Taiwan, a place of love.

Yayoi Kusama

序

黃才郎

國立台灣美術館館長

生命的足跡
複合媒材，保麗龍雕塑與聚氨酯塗料
尺寸可變
2010

Footprints of Life
mixed media, styrofoam sculptures with urethane paintdimension
variable
2010

今年3月，國立臺灣美術館戶外廣場迎來了一場彩色圓點的視覺盛宴，日本當代藝術家草間彌生的創作〈生命的足跡〉（Footprints of Life, 2010），在綠意盎然的草坪上，以十五組件的桃紅有機雕塑，展現出跌宕起伏生命律動，這件作品曾在不同的城市展出，與展出地的地景人文共融出獨一無二的美學內蘊，記錄著草間彌生一場場不同旅程的生命足跡，如今短暫留駐於此，與美術館園區常設展出的臺灣當代雕塑作品相互輝映，靜美地等待著觀者細細品味。

草間彌生（Yayoi Kusama, 1929~），被英國《泰晤士報》評選為「二十世紀最偉大的藝術家」之一，在創作風格上難以界定流派。卻在國際藝壇上有著舉足輕重的地位，她曾描述自己僅是一位「執念藝術家」（obsessive artist），然其創作前衛大膽，不拘泥於任何形式，不受他人影響，始終堅持著自己的藝術方向。2011至2012年間，英國泰特美術館（TATE Modern）為草間彌生舉辦了個人大型回顧展，並於馬德里、巴黎、倫敦、紐約四地的當代藝術殿堂巡迴展出，讓她成為躍上世界舞台的首位日本女性頂尖藝術家。

草間彌生讓人感佩之處，莫過於那份對藝術的堅定，雖已年過八旬，仍堅持每天創作，向世人傳達她內心「愛與和平」的幸福語意。「圓點」是草間彌生最重要的藝術標記，「鏡射」則是她慣用的視覺形式，在看似繽紛奇幻的藝術語彙裡，實則蘊含著藝術家的自我救贖。其自幼深受幻聽與幻視所苦，藉由描繪圓點的複製與增殖，肯定自我的價值，在日本傳統社會與家庭的文化禁錮中，草間彌生透過藝術擺脫羈絆，在毛遂自薦地寫信給美國藝術家喬治亞·歐姬芙（Georgia O'Keeffe）的機緣下，1957年11月18日踏上攸關命運的赴美之路，動身前，她將數百張畫作燒毀，代表著自己與過去訣別與迎向未來的決心。

60年代的草間彌生以作品〈無限的網〉（Infinity Nets）一舉震撼了紐約藝壇，與當時盛行的抽象表現主義截然不同，巨大的畫布上呈現出無數細微的網點，嚴謹中挑撥觀者心中的靜謐。隨後她的觸角伸及立體作品、肢體表演、電影與時尚等領域，創作涵蓋超現實主義、抽象表現主義、極簡主義、普普藝術、行為藝術等多元觀念與形式；而至60年代後期，她更跳脫畫廊與美術館的範疇，在街頭或廣場等公共空間發表作品，積極推動「偶發藝術」，舉辦人體彩繪、時尚走秀、派對等，引起媒體騷動，藉由藝術創作傳達對現有社會制度的不滿。

1966年草間彌生於第三十三屆威尼斯雙年展，發表作品〈自戀庭園〉（Narcissus Garden），未受到官方邀請的她，決定自行參展的方式，用1500顆現成工業產品的的塑膠銀球，鋪滿於義大利國家館外的戶外草坪，用一顆兩元美金的低價向觀眾兜售，藉此批判藝術的商業主義，此舉造成轟動但也被主辦單位裝置展初期期間禁止。直至1993年，草間彌生正式以日本代表的身分參加第四十五屆威尼斯雙年展，也獲得國際藝術界的許多正面評價，90年代的歐美雜誌曾給予其評論，「草間彌生長年來隱姓埋名躲藏在自己無垠的世界當中，終於在這後現代的歷史時刻，為了伸張她的定位而重新現身。」

饒富故事性與啟發性的作品〈自戀庭園〉（Narcissus Garden）亦為本次草間彌生亞洲巡展作品之一，展示於本館下凹庭園，同樣在綠地之上藍天之下，卻異於60年代的藝術氛圍，半世紀後的人們對於草間彌生行為藝術的充分理解，讓欣賞作品的思維更加開闊，同時亦更能認同威尼斯雙年展的成功在草間彌生創作生涯的重要性。

「夢我所夢：草間彌生亞洲巡迴展」臺灣站將於國立臺灣美術館劃下完美的句點，謹此向本次草間彌生亞洲巡迴展臺灣站的各主辦單位日本草間彌生工作室（KUSAMA Enterprise）、大田畫廊（Ota Fine Arts）、高雄市立美術館、旺旺中時媒體集團時藝多媒體與三立集團閣林文創，以及亞洲巡迴展總策展人韓國大邱美術館金善姬館長（Ms. Kim Sunhee）致意，亦向台新銀行等各協辦與贊助單位敬致謝忱，承蒙各單位的專業付出與協力合作，方能使得展覽在臺順利圓滿。

黃才郎

2015年6月

Foreword

Huang Tsai-Lang

Director of National Taiwan Museum of Fine Arts

This March, a visual feast of colorful polka dots came to the outdoor courtyard of National Taiwan Museum of Fine Arts (NTMoFA). On the green lawn, *Footprints of Life* (2010) created by Japanese contemporary artist Yayoi Kusama showcase the ups and downs of the rhythm of life through fifteen pink sculptures in organic forms. This set of sculptures has been exhibited in different cities and blended with local landscapes and cultures to form unique aesthetic connotations, chronicling Yayoi Kusama's footprints of life over various journeys. During their temporary stay, the sculptures resonate with the Taiwanese contemporary sculptures in the museum's permanent collection, calmly and gracefully awaiting visitors to admire and savor them.

Yayoi Kusama (1929~) has been chosen by British newspaper The Times as one of "The 200 Greatest Artists in the Twentieth Century." Her creative style cannot be categorized into any school; nonetheless, she enjoys prestigious status in the international art circle. She once described herself as an "obsessive artist," and her works are bold and edgy, unbounded by any formality, nor influenced by other people. She has always persisted in her own artistic direction. From 2011 to 2012, Tate Modern in London hosted Yayoi Kusama's retrospective exhibition, which toured four major global centers of contemporary art, Madrid, Paris, London, and New York, confirming the status of the first female Japanese artist who leaped onto the global stage.

Yayoi Kusama impresses us the most by her dedication to art. Well beyond the age of 80 now, she still insists on working everyday, spreading to people in the world the messages of happiness that come from the "love and peace" in her heart. "Polka dot motif" is Yayoi Kusama's most important artistic symbol, and "mirror reflection" is her typical visual form; her seemingly colorful and fantasy-like artistic vocabulary actually embodies the artist's self-salvation. Yayoi Kusama suffers from acousma and heteroptics since an early age, and through duplication and reproduction of polka dots, she affirms her own value. Through art, Yayoi Kusama has broken free from the cultural shackles of traditional Japanese society and family. After writing letters to Georgia O'Keefe, she embarked on the fateful journey to the United States on November 18, 1957. Before she left Japan, she burned hundreds of her own paintings into ashes, which represented her determination to bid farewell to the past and move on towards the future.

Yayoi Kusama took the New York art scene by surprise in the 1960s with her work Infinity Nets. Unlike the popular abstract expressionism at the time, her giant canvases displayed countless meshes of net, which meticulously teased the inner tranquility of spectators. Later on, she ventured into three-dimensional works, performance art, movie, and even fashion; her creative works encompass diverse concepts and forms, including surrealism, abstract expressionism, minimalism, pop art, and performance art. In the late 1960s, she even broke the boundaries of galleries and museums, and showcased her works in public spaces—in the streets or public squares—as she actively promoted Happening Art. She organized body painting events, fashion shows, and parties, creating much buzz in the media, and expressed her dissatisfaction of the existing social system through art.

In 1966, Yayoi Kusama exhibited her work *Narcissus Garden* at the 33rd Venice Biennale. Without an official invitation, she decided to appear at the Biennale guerrilla-style; she spread 1,500 plastic silver balls, a readymade industrial product, over the lawn outside of the Italian Pavilion, and sold the balls to spectators at a price of US$ 2 each, to show her criticism of art commercialism. Her action created quite a stir, and was immediately prohibited by the organizer while the installation itself was exhibited during the biennale. In 1993, Yayoi Kusama represented Japan in the 45th Venice Biennale and gained favorable reviews from the global art circle. "Yayoi Kusama has lived unknown in her boundless world for years, and finally, at this historic moment of postmodernism, she reappears to claim her place," described European and American art magazines.

Narcissus Garden, a narrative and inspiring work, will also be exhibited at this touring exhibition of Yayoi Kusama. It will be displayed at NTMoFA's courtyard, and once again appear on green lawn under the bright blue sky; however, the atmosphere will be nothing like that of the 1960s. Half a century later, people now fully understand Yayoi Kusama's performance art, so they will be more open-minded when looking at her works, and recognize the significance of her success at the Venice Biennale to her creative career.

Kusama Yayoi, A Dream I Dreamed makes its final stop in Taiwan at National Taiwan Museum of Fine Arts. I'd like to express my greatest appreciation to the organizers of this Yayoi Kusama touring exhibition: KUSAMA Enterprise, Ota Fine Arts, Kaohsiung Museum of Fine Arts, Media Sphere Communications of Want Want China Times Inc., and Greenland International Books of Sanli Media Group; the curator of the touring exhibition, Director Kim Sunhee of Daegu Art Museum; and Taishin International Bank and other co-organizers and sponsors. Thanks to your professional effort and collaboration, this exhibition has successfully arrived in Taichung, Taiwan.

2015, June

關於草間彌生展

金善姬

大邱市立美術館館長

首先對於此次在台灣的國立台灣美術館（台中）以及高雄市立美術館能舉辦草間彌生的個展感到無限欣喜。此次展覽為草間彌生的亞洲巡迴展，從韓國的大邱市立美術館首展，再巡迴至上海、首爾，接著來到台灣，之後還會繼續前往印度等地展出。期待這次的台灣巡迴展，也能像所有草間展覽舉辦的地點一樣令人喜悅和特別。

2013年能舉辦草間彌生展覽，實在是非常幸運。大邱市立美術館雖然是嶄新的美術館，具有大型的展覽設施，然而或許因位於遠離都市的地方，參觀人數有限。透過舉辦草間彌生展覽，大邱市立美術館不僅迅速成名，參觀人數也有爆發性的成長。目前大邱市立美術館幾乎無人不曉，美術館的觀眾也絡繹不絕。更驚人的是不僅是大邱市立美術館，其他巡迴地的美術館，也有了超越本館的成果。對於不熟悉當代藝術的韓國或亞洲的一般大眾，以及對當代藝術感興趣的觀眾而言，草間展成為一樣特別的禮物。

草間彌生被評為足以代表我們這個時代的頂尖藝術家。來自亞洲的女性藝術家得到這樣的評價，讓草間彌生的生活不再平淡。她在過去60年來面臨了無數的困境，以藝術家的身份度過精彩的生活。更重要的是就算是身處逆境，她依然開拓出新的藝術概念和新的媒材，不斷地拓展藝術的領域。此外，她具有別人無法仿效的創意和神秘，憑直覺創造出充滿能量且另人感動的藝術世界。比較廣為人知的是黃色南瓜和圓點圖案，然而至今為止，草間彌生創作了無數的作品。有繪畫、雕塑、前衛藝術活動、媒體藝術，甚至還有時尚，不僅種類繁多，素材也很豐富。想到草間彌生豐富的藝術泉源，不由得令人感到驚奇不已。她的藝術是超越所有存在的生與滅的神聖世界，其中訴說著藝術起源的故事。她的藝術展現了宇宙的混沌，混沌中還蘊含了規則與重覆的韻律，創作出違反重力浮游的時間、深邃的海洋，還有廣袤的宇宙空間。那是融合圖案、色彩和光線的世界，消除了外緣的界線，變化成無限擴大的空間，而觀眾則受邀進入這種令人難以抗拒的空間。

觀眾會跟著陷入一種未曾經歷過的心理狀態，就彷彿初生的孩子。近期作品當中，片段、零碎的圖像，有如壁畫上的古代神話一般，任意用敘述的方式重現記錄，引人遐思，激發無限想像。草間彌生的作品雖然是在一個框架內組成，但卻能從既有藝術的具象結構裡的傳統元素中解放。更重要的是其豐富的涵義超越了語言。因此，無論男女老少，抑或是文化背景不同的異邦人，都能瞭解她的作品，毫無限制或約束之感。她的作品既具普遍性，又含有超越性的力量。因此，草間的藝術展現出：藝術的本質無法以理法（言語、理論）加以表現；反之，如欲以言語闡述，則將失去藝術的本質。

在草間彌生無數的繪畫、雕塑、裝置作品中，〈無限的網〉（*Infinity Nets*）、〈圓點執念〉（*Dots Obsession*）、〈無限鏡屋〉（*Infinity Mirrored Room*）系列作品被視為其主要創作，這些作品呈現草間的藝術探索，包括對於現實與虛無，有限與無限，生命與死亡的探究。這些主題和她罹患的偏執症心理狀態有關。實際上，她從小就罹患了偏執性強迫症，她的病症和藝術有著密不可分的連結。藝術家在自己的作品中將相同的形狀或視覺元素重複、增加、擴散，揮灑出自己腦海裡的圖案。藝術家的強迫症或幻想症成為其藝術創作的根基，而藝術則成為其病症的治療工具。草間的藝術創作為人指點迷津，走向有意義的藝術世界，同時也成為藝術家本人，以及所有現代人逃離不安、壓抑與執念的避難處。雖然是比較沉重的主題，然而草間的作品卻相當單純明快。神秘而深邃、卻又強烈而華麗。草間曾表示，如果有一天可以用一句話描述自己的作品，那應該可以說是「追求幸福」吧！相信人們也會有同感。草間作品中所散發的味道，就是「幸福」。幸福是藝術家和我們所有人嚮往之處。

草間彌生目前86歲，經常往返於醫院與工作室之間，不過卻尚未停止創作，總是神采奕奕地投入創作。她的藝術泉源不會乾枯，總是源源不絕地湧出。每次見到她時，她都會說：「因為還能創作，所以非常幸福，因此到死去的那一刻也不會放下畫筆。」，透過藝術，她不僅克服了疾病，還戰勝了長期以來的家庭問題與生活上的痛苦。對她而言，她的人生就是身為藝術家。就如同草間的自白，我認為她的藝術和她的生活已結為一體。因此這次展覽的所有觀眾，就成了草間藝術的幸福的巡禮者，從她的藝術得到嶄新豐富的靈感，並且長時間延續下去。

為了這次的展覽，從日本等世界各地運來包含舊作和新作的共110多件作品，運輸份量相當可觀。這次的展覽能成形，除了要特別感謝為本展覽熱情創作新作品的藝術家，以及對於安排、協助作品借展等艱辛繁雜的工作，不吝給予所有支援的草間彌生工作室小組和大田畫廊（Ota Fine Arts），對於每位在這複雜艱難的展覽準備過程中給予支援的人士，在此也獻上最真摯的謝意。

2015年1月

On the Kusama Yayoi's Exhibition

Kim Sunhee

Director, Daegu Art Museum

First of all, I am very pleased that National Taiwan Museum of Fine Arts (Taichung) and Kaohsiung Museum of Fine Arts are hosting Kusama Yayoi's solo exhibition. This exhibition is part of her Asian travelling show that started from the Daegu Art Museum of Korea and travelled to Shanghai and Seoul, now making its stop at Taiwan. The exhibition will also continue to travel to India. I expect that Kusama's show in Taiwan will be as special and auspicious as it had been in all its previous exhibition venues.

I was, in fact, very fortunate to be able to realize Kusama Yayoi's exhibition in 2013 at the museum. Daegu Art Museum is a newly-opened beautiful museum equipped with large-scale exhibition facilities, and yet it did not attract a very impressive audience, most likely because of its location outside the main downtown area. However the Kusama Yayoi exhibition made Daegu Art Museum become very famous and at the same time saw an explosive increase in audience size. The museum has been widely known and publicized; our museum is now almost a household name and always filled with visitors. What is more, other museums to which Kusama's show travelled equally had huge successes. Kusama Yayoi exhibition turned out to be an extraordinary present for many Asian audiences, whether they still feel unfamiliar with contemporary art or are already attuned to contemporary art with great interest and concern.

Kusama Yayoi has been acknowledged as one of the greatest artists to represent our times. Her life was never an easy and smooth path until she achieved the credit of an internationally recognized Asian female artist. Kusama has been intensely committed to her artistic life, confronting countless hardships for over 60 years. Her great strength is, above all, to untiringly push the artistic parameter forward by exploring new concepts and media of art, in spite of many adversities in life. At the same time, she succeeded to formulate an artistic realm that is unique, mysterious, intuitive and powerful, surpassing anyone's imitation. The dotted pumpkins and polka dot patterns are the most well-known to the public but she has been creating a diverse gamut of work. She has worked on paintings, sculptures and media art, and was engaged in performance art and Happenings, as well as fashion designing. Kusama's creative subject matters seemed to know no limit. One cannot but be surprised at the source of her rich creation. Her art refers to the transcendental realm related to the birth and perishing of all beings; within her art is a narrative of the origin of art. Through her art, one encounters the chaos of the universe where the rhythm of regulations and their repetition is contained within. Kusama's universe alters itself to time that defies gravity, and this space of the universe is sometimes expressed as a deep sea through her art. It is a world where patterns, colors and light are intermingled whilst its outer boundary gets diminished and thus the perimeter infinitely is induced to expand – the audience is invited into this overwhelming space.

The audience could fall into this special psychological state that a child could have been in from an immemorial time; a state that had never been experienced before. In her recent works, the fragmented symbols are represented and recorded in a similar way to the ancient mythologies in frescos: they are heavily evocative, driving us to impulsive imagination. Although Kusama's works are composed within a single frame, they are free from the conventional elements of representational structure found in previous art. The most striking is that the rich implication of her works transcends language. There is no limit or constraint in understanding her works in terms of age, gender, or cultural difference. What is both universal and transcendental is the power of her art. In this light, Kusama's art illuminates the nature of art that cannot be expressed by words and logic, revealing to us that on the contrary,the nature of art could be lost if expressed by words.

I consider *"Infinity Nets"*, *"Dots Obsession"* and *"Infinity Mirrored Room"* series are her main works among the vast array of works of paintings, sculptures or installations. Kusama's artistic concern that manifests through such works, therefore, encompasses an exploration of reality and fiction, the finite and the infinite, life and death. Such themes are related to the artist's psychological state of obsessive-compulsive disorder since childhood; her chronic disease and her own art have been inseparable. She herself said that the patterns or visual elements that repeat, propagate and diffuse in her work are what she regurgitates from her own head that is full of images. In other words, it suggests that the artist's obsessive-compulsive disorder or hallucinosis was foundational in her art-making and in turn, the art was instrumental in the curing of her disease. Her art-making indicates an exit towards the world of art that is meaningful and at the same time offers itself as a shelter for all modern human beings from anxiety, oppression and obsession. Despite the fact that the works deal with issues that are somewhat heavy, they unfold themselves in an unexpectedly simple and lucid way. It is all the more mysterious and deep whilst being intense and dazzling. She once claimed that her own art could be encapsulated into" the search for happiness". I believe the viewers will agree with her. It is because what is being celebrated inside her art is happiness itself. After all, happiness is the ultimate purpose in life that everyone including the artist wishes for.

Kusama, currently 86 years old, shuttles between the hospital and the studio but is still actively engaged in making art. Her artistic spring is ceaselessly surging and far from being exhaustible. Every time I meet her, she says to me: "I am so happy because I can work. I will never abandon the brush until the last moment of death" She also adds that she was able to stand up against her own chronic disease, conflicts with her family and hardships in life through art and she lives purely as an artist. I am convinced that Kusama's art and personal life is one, just as she confesses. The audience who come are the pilgrims and their journey through Kusama's exhibition will be their pilgrimage. In this process, the audience will achieve the kind of happiness that Kusama did through her art. The refreshing and lavish inspiration of Kusama's art will never fade easily.

Approximately 110 pieces of works, both previous and recent, were gathered for this exhibition from all corners of the globe. The sheer scale of transportation was huge. I express my heartfelt thanks to the artist herself who passionately made new works for this exhibition, the members of Kusama's studio team and the Ota Fine Arts who did not hesitate to go through all the countless trouble and complicated procedures for locating and requesting the loan of the artworks. Realizing the exhibition was not an easy task from the very beginning. My sincere gratitude goes to everyone who provided any and every form of assistance in making this exhibition a success.

2015, February

夢我所夢　眾享所愛

蔡紹中

旺旺中時媒體集團總裁

「圓點女王」草間彌生，終於來到臺灣！

從南瓜、圓點到鏡射世界，草間彌生的圓點魔力早在臺灣的時尚界、藝文界、建築界蔓延。回顧其創作原初，圓點從她自身對生命、社會控訴的符號，到成為領導世界大眾追隨的標幟。草間彌生經過多次反覆的考驗與挑戰，始終忠於本我、追隨執念；她的執念成就了藝術，而她的藝術是她生命的泉源、永恆的愛。

《夢我所夢：草間彌生亞洲巡迴展》是草間彌生在亞洲首度的巡迴個展，自2013年起至2014年巡迴韓國大邱、上海、首爾等地皆締造口碑與熱潮。草間彌生本人非常重視這個展覽，不但親自參與挑選作品，更特地為這個亞洲巡迴展繪製新作，可見她對本展的重視。

本次特展以全面且多元的方式呈現草間驚人的藝術爆發力，包含裝置、雕刻、繪畫以及影像等近120件草間近年的全新創作與經典作品，是台灣草間彌生個展的空前首例。策展人以瀰漫空間的圓球、無限蔓延的繽紛圓點、如幻似真的鏡像反射、巨大的南瓜、花朵與狗兒、綺麗多彩而引人遐思的圖像……構築草間彌生的夢中奇境，一層一層帶領著觀眾一步一步走進草間彌生的藝術世界，感受圓點聚散之間帶給她的悲與喜、真與假、是與非。

特別感謝策展人韓國大邱市立美術館金善姬（KiM Sunhee）館長、大田畫廊（Ota Fine Arts）以及日本草間彌生工作室（KUSAMA Enterprice）將臺灣作為亞洲巡迴展的一環，並感謝國立臺灣美術館、三立集團閣林文創能與旺旺中時媒體集團時藝多媒體共同合作，以及台新銀行的贊助，一起深耕當代藝術教育，帶給台灣民眾新的藝術視野和體驗。

草間彌生：「我透過藝術感受到生命真切的美好，世界藝術的不朽魅力總能撼動我心，這是唯一帶給我希望的地方，並讓我沒有遺憾。這也是我所生活的方式，並將是我繼續生存的方向。」一百年後，世界的人們終將繼續追尋草間彌生的方向，持續傾倒於她的圓點幻夢。

A Dream I Dreamed:
Let Everyone Enjoy What They Love

President of Want Want China Times Media Group

The "Queen of Dots" has finally come to Taiwan!

Kusama Yayoi has been known for her pumpkins, dots and mirror-reflection artworks and her power in making dots had constantly spread and influenced Taiwan's fashion, art, and architecture. The dots had originally from a symbol of self-redemption then became a world-leading fashion symbol. After she met the repetitionary challenges, she persists in herself that makes her achieved in art field as art is her life spring and eternal love.

"Kusama Yayoi, A Dream I Dreamed" is Kusama Yayoi's first major touring exhibition in Asia. This exhibition had raised a burst of upsurge while touring in Shanghai, Daegu and Seoul from 2013 to 2014 . To show her attention in this exhibition, Kusama had not only selected artworks but also created new works specially for this touring exhibiton.

The touring exhibition will display on a large scale Kusama Yayoi's art including nearly 120 remarkable art creation, from her recent years. Shown in Taiwan for the first time. The curator represents Kusama Yayoi's dreamland by spreading hundred dots over, replicating colorful dots infinitely, utilizing virtual mirror reflection, illustrating gigantic pumpkins, flowers, dogs, gorgeously colors and illusive images. It leads the audience into Kusama Yayoi's artistic world gradually. Among rhythmic dots, people can experience her sorrow and joy, reality and ideality.

Special thanks to the exhibition curator KiM Sunhee, director of the Daegu Art Museum, Ota Fine Arts, and Kusama Enterprise for planning Taiwan as a stop in the Asian tour. Many thanks to the National Taiwan Museum of Fine Arts and Greenland Creative Co., Ltd. for cooperating with Media Sphere Communication Ltd., Want Want China Times Media Group to give the people of Taiwan a chance to broaden their life. Last, thanks to Taishin Bank for the sponsorship that promotes the contemporary art education and gives local people a chance to enrich their cultural life.

Kusama Yayoi, " I feel how truly wonderful life is, and I tremble with undying fascination for the world of art, the only place that gives me hope and will have no regrets. This is the way I have lived my life, and it is the way I shall go on living." A century later, people worldwide would continue to have a deep love for Kusama Yayoi's dots wonderland.

被英國《泰晤士報》評選為「二十世紀最偉大的藝術家」之一的草間彌生，在日本獲獎不斷，是相當重要的當代藝術家，也曾獲頒美國終身成就獎、法國藝術及文學騎士勳章等殊榮，從平面的繪畫創作、雕刻到裝置藝術，她的創作風格獨特、多元，無人所及。

自幼即立志當藝術家的草間，從小為精神幻覺所苦，繪畫是其自我救贖的良方。今日，她的作品仍不斷於世界各地展出，並被多所知名美術館所典藏，她從沒想過，為了克服幻覺恐懼，自我消融的圓點，時至今日會成為她征服世界的利器！

在各界引頸期盼下，2015年《夢我所夢：草間彌生亞洲巡迴展》（KUSAMA YAYOI, A Dream I Dreamed）正式在台灣高雄與台中兩地登場，展覽涵蓋草間彌生跨度60年的經典創作元素與搶眼新作，是台灣草間彌生個展的空前首例。

展覽以全面且多元的方式呈現草間彌生驚人的藝術創作脈絡，從讓人感受草間絢爛魔力的代表作〈曼哈頓自殺慣犯之歌〉（Songofa Manhattan Suicide Addict）、〈無限鏡屋〉（Infinity Mirrored Room），到最為人熟知的〈南瓜〉（Pumpkin），以繽紛色彩、重複圓點堆砌而成的，包含裝置，雕刻，繪畫以及影像等近120件作品，綜合勾勒出草間彌生的藝術創作生涯，引領觀眾透過展覽一同深入全球矚目的草間世界！

閣林文創長期以來一直致力於藝術文化的推廣，期能讓「藝術生活化，生活藝術化」，這次很榮幸的能夠參與這次的盛事，讓民眾不用出國，就能欣賞國際級的藝術精華，也感謝所有參與此展的團隊夥伴。我們相信通過此次展覽的舉辦，將能帶給民眾不一樣的視野，豐富民眾的文化生活，讓藝術人文的種子傳播到每個人心中。

楊培中

Foreword

Pei-Chung Yang

General Manager of Greenland Creative CO., Ltd.

Kusama Yayoi, who was born in Japan's Nagano Prefecture in 1929, has been acclaimed "one of the greatest artists of the 20th century" by The London Times, and is highly considered as a very public figure in Japan with numbers of awards. She has won the America's Lifetime Achievement Award and France's Ordre des Arts et des Lettres. She has brought a style that is unique, varied, and inimitable to paintings, sculpture, and installation art.

Kusama, who set her mind on becoming an artist at a very young age, suffered from hallucinations and mental instability since childhood, and she found that painting brought her a sense of self-redemption. Today, Kusama Yayoi's works are exhibited continuously around the world, and have been collected by around hundred art museums. Kusama never expected that the self-annihilating dots she created to overcome the fear of her hallucinations would become the weapons with which she would conquer the world!

With the much anticipated in Taiwan, "Kusama Yayoi, A Dream I Dreamed" is held in Kaohsiung and Taichung in 2015. The exhibition includes Kusama Yayoi's significant masterpieces over sixty years and eye-catching works painted in these three years. It is Kusama Yayoi's first-ever solo exhibition in Taiwan.

The exhibition will present the context of Kusama Yayoi's astonishing creativity in a comprehensive and far-reaching manner. Works will range from Kusama's magical "Song of a Manhattan Suicide Addict" and "Infinity Mirrored Room" to the very well-known "Pumpkin." The exhibition will include close to 120 works, including installations, sculptures, paintings, and video, and will feature her characteristically dazzling colors and use of infinitely repeating dots. Apart from providing an overview of Kusama Yayoi's artistic career, the exhibition will bring viewers into Kusama's own personal world.

Greenland Creative Co., Ltd. has been constantly in promoting art and culture, and hope to create "Art is life; Life is art." It is our honor to participate in this grand event. Such magnificent opportunity makes the public could enjoy the world-class art without going abroad. We profoundly appreciate to all of the team members who join to organize this exhibition. We believe that people could broaden their horizon, enrich their cultural life, and plant the seeds of art and culture in everyone's hearts by engaging Kusama Yayoi's exhibition.

草間彌生築夢的藝術人生

陸蓉之

草間彌生1929年3月22日，出生於日本長野縣松本市的一戶殷實家庭，她的不尋常的童年生活，夾在父母親不信任的婚姻關係之間，同時飽受母親的偏激和強勢的對待，使她甚至產生輕生的意圖。繪畫，是草間彌生的生命救贖與無盡想像出口。十歲的時候她用鉛筆畫的母親畫像，整個畫面上就已經覆蓋了大大小小的圓點，這些圓點日後成為了她的創作符號與個人標記。草間彌生從家鄉長野縣松本第一女子高校畢業以後，到京都就讀於市立工藝美術學校，主修的是日本畫，為她奠定了繪畫的基礎訓練。

青年時代的草間彌生，其實已經展現了她在藝術方面的才華，1949年才20歲的她，畫的一幅〈殘夢〉（*Lingering Dream*）入選日本第二屆創作獎。然而她和母親的關係並未獲得改善，性格偏執的母親完全不能理解或欣賞女兒的藝術天分，反而再三阻擾女兒的藝術追求，刺激了草間彌生產生離家遠赴重洋的念想。放洋出國，對那個時代的日本女性而言，真是非常大膽和前衛的想法。

由於草間彌生的創作是出自於她本能的需求和存在狀態的自然反射，這種天才型的藝術家，往往不受外界環境的影響，也不會在意所謂的時代風貌或藝術風格的承傳。草間彌生的創造力來自於她藝術的天賦和她的獨特經驗。她曾經如此描述：「有一天我看著紅色桌布上的花案，等我抬起頭時，我看到同樣的紅花圖案滿布在天花板、窗戶和牆壁上，最後彌漫了整個房間，我的身體，整個宇宙。我感覺我好像開始自我消融，在無限的時間和絕對的空間裡旋轉著，直到我被消滅成為虛無。我意識到這一切正在發生，不僅僅是我的想像，我嚇得只知道自己一定要逃走，免得我被紅色花朵的魔咒剝奪了我的人生。我拼命地跑上樓，然而我下面的樓梯開始崩解，我從樓梯摔了下來，扭傷了我的腳踝。」此時「自我消融」的概念已經成形，從此深植於她的創作思維裡。

決心要出國的草間彌生，寫信給當時的法國總統，表達她想要去法國的心願，竟然得到他的回信，告知她得去法國大使館申請文化交流的專案，而且必須通過法語的測試才能成行。草間彌生開始學習法語，甚至得到了在巴黎一所藝術學校的入學許可，但是她為了準備幾個在東京的個展，迫使她推遲了前往法國。後來她在舊書店裡看到喬治亞·歐姬芙（Georgia O'Keeffe）的畫冊，聽説她是美國很有名的藝術家，為了寫信給她，草間彌生搭了6個小時火車到東京的美國大使館，在名人錄裡找到了歐姬芙的聯繫方式，開始了她和歐姬芙之間的通信往來，也總算實際邁出了她千方百計出國的一步。

赴美前，草間彌生在當地的河流邊燒毀了她數百件作品，為了顯示她下定決心要離開日本，在一個未知的土地上開創新成就的意志。她在1957年的時候獲得佐伊度三（Zoe Dusanne）畫廊的邀請，是西雅圖一間著名的現代藝術畫廊，安排她在那裡舉辦個展，草間彌生終於飛向了美國。此時艾爾弗雷德·史蒂格勒茲（Alfred Stieglitz）已經去世，歐姬芙搬到了新墨西哥，但是仍為草間彌生寫了推薦信，後來還特意與她相見。草間彌生在西雅圖展出後，在1958年移居紐約。初到紐約的生活極其困苦，尤其在冬天，饑寒交迫，幾至貧病交加，生計無以為繼。在如此艱難的環境裡，繪畫依然是她最大的救贖，這個時期發展出巨幅的〈無限的網〉（Infinity Nets）系列繪畫，如今已經成為她的經典代表作。

1959年唐納德·賈德（Donald Judd）一位藝術家也是《藝術新聞》（*ART news*）的藝評人，他評論〈無限的網〉的論點非常精闢：「那效果既複雜又簡單，主要是由兩個靠近而幾乎平行的平面交互作用而成…在表層的交會點和其他分離之處，些微但強而有力。」[①]

而草間彌生對她自己的創作則有如下的説法：「消蝕和積累，傳播與分離，從宇宙迴旋而來的消融與無狀微粒，都變得不那麼魅魔，而是我的藝術的基礎，在這時便已經成形。」[②]

戰後的美國紐約取代法國巴黎成為全球的藝術中心，抽象表現主義正在勢頭上，普普藝術才開始萌發，草間彌生作為極少數在紐約活動的亞洲女性藝術家，她很快受到了關注。她的精神狀態使她總是能夠極為專注於她想做的事，而且無所畏懼，例如她可以不眠不休連續畫40到50個小時，她有能力號召數百人由她來指揮的行為藝術，她膽敢寫公開信給美國總統尼克森（Richard Nixon）宣示她的反戰立場，要美國總統立即終止越戰。她總是按照自己的意志行事，使她的任何藝術創作都充滿了原型的魅力和原創的力量。她的單色〈無限的網〉看起來像是極簡主義的作品，卻發生在極簡運動之前；她使用複數圖像做的裝置作品，比安迪‧沃荷（Andy Warhol）還早；而她縫製許多陽具的裝置作品，更是在克勒斯‧歐登伯格（Claes Oldenburg）的軟雕塑之前。她自由自在的選用五花八門的媒材來創作，包括了人體；形式也不曾受到任何拘束，從繪畫、雕塑、裝置藝術、行為藝術、攝影、電影、錄影、服裝設計、寫作…，幾乎涉獵了所有可以想得到創作形式。

今日，回顧草間彌生從1950年代末期到美國紐約以來的創作發展，她一直是一位無拘無束的天生原創者。她1960年代的裝置作品和行為藝術，經常透露強烈的女性意識，然而她和美國1970年代的女性運動卻一點關係也沒有，而且也是她的藝術發生在那運動之前。她的女性主義傾向，單純地因為她以作品淋漓盡致演繹了她的人生，而她是一位女性而已。她像歷史中一些偉大的藝術家一樣，他們將自己的人生幻化成藝術的本身。

1960年代在紐約是草間彌生創作火力全開的關鍵時期，站在當代藝術最前線闖出自己一片天地。草間彌生的偏執性強迫症使得她具有超越凡人的創造力與生產力，她在紐約，亟欲出名，可以讓她載譽歸國，她所作的全方位出擊，無論是作品的多元與多量，都令人覺得不可思議，更是亞洲藝術家當中絕對無出其右者。

她在1959年就已經獲邀參加一些團體展，並且舉辦個展，然而1960年她被邀請參加德國市立美術館（Städtisches Museum）舉辦的一項《單色繪畫》（Monochrome Malerei）國際大展，她和馬克‧羅斯科(Mark Rothko)是從紐約獲邀的唯二藝術家。這時草間彌生已經和盧齊歐‧封塔納（Lucio Fontana）、伊伏‧克萊因（Yves Klein）、皮耶羅‧曼佐尼（Piero Manzoni）和岡瑟‧尤克（Günther Uecker）這些歐洲重量級的前衛藝術家同台，次年被惠特尼美術館（Whitney Museum of American Art）邀請參加《1961惠特尼年度展》（1961 Whitney Annual）（惠特尼雙年展的前身），這樣的成就超越了當時任何來自亞洲的藝術家。更令人難以想像的是日後宣稱「繪畫已經死亡」，當時是藝評家的唐納‧賈德不但分期付款買了草間彌生的〈無限的網〉，而且在草間彌生搬進同棟大樓以後，他們更成為好友，在草間彌生製作軟雕塑時，賈德還經常去幫忙並鼓勵她。

1962年6月在紐約格林畫廊舉辦的一個團體展當中，草間彌生獲邀參加，第一次發表了她的軟雕塑〈積累〉（Accumulation）系列，同時參展的還有克勒斯‧歐登柏格、詹姆斯‧羅森奎斯特（James Rosenquist）、喬治‧席格爾（George Segal）和安迪‧沃荷等人，這個展覽日後被譽為第一個普普藝術的展覽。當時克勒斯‧歐登柏格展出的僅是一套處理過西服，而草間彌生綴滿布縫製陽具的沙發和座椅，令眾人驚歎，克勒斯‧歐登柏格不可能沒看到，等到那年秋季他推出的個展，打出軟雕塑的旗號，使他立即在國際間成名，卻否認受到草間彌生的啟發，她所期待的格林畫廊捨棄她反而與克勒斯‧歐登柏格簽約，應該是刺激草間彌生痼疾復發的重要原因之一。在封閉自己的環境中，草間彌生的創作並未停滯，她在1963年發表〈積聚：千舟連翩〉（Aggregation: One Thousand Boat Show），在一間房裡同時展現了她的軟雕塑和複數圖像的大型裝置，說明了一切。

草間彌生宣稱自己是第一位「執念藝術家」，她對男性和性的恐懼，反而促成她製作了鋪天蓋地的陽具形象和物件。從〈無限的網〉的平面繪畫蔓延到空間裡，打破了空間和媒材的限制，運用現成物和攝影圖片，製作大量的軟雕塑，裝置藝術見證了她的創造力再度爆發，使用鏡面的交互無盡反射，真正把「無限的網」延伸到了無限的空間，1965年她展出了〈無限鏡屋-陽具的原野〉（Infinity Mirrored Room-Phalli's Field），1966年的《草間彌生的窺探秀》（Kusama's Peep Show）更完善了她利用鏡面反射的創作技法，鏡屋裝置成為草間彌生藝術的另一個符號。

1966年草間彌生自嘲以「突擊」的手法參加了第33屆威尼斯雙年展，發表了她的〈自戀庭園〉（*Narcissus Garden*），她將1500只鏡球鋪滿義大利館門前的兩片草地，當她穿了華麗的和服，以「你的自戀」名義，開始在現場以每一個1,200里拉的價格（大約2美元）販售她的鏡球，立刻引起雙年展主委會的注意，禁止她在雙年展進行商業販售的行為。這個不愉快的事件，終於在27年後獲得平反，草間彌生風光地回到雙年展的現場，她在一間全是鏡面的房間裡，反覆反射無限重複黃底黑圓點的大型裝置，她也穿了特製的黃底黑圓點連身長裙，帶著尖尖的同花色的高帽子，出現在展覽會場，吸睛指數爆表，她甚至親自在門口跟觀眾致意，分送小南瓜，參觀者在日本館門前大排長龍，成為那一年威尼斯雙年展風頭最健的藝術家。

然而，草間彌生的夢魘還是如影隨形，1966年10月盧卡斯・薩馬拉斯在紐約一流的大畫廊推出他的〈鏡屋〉（*Mirror-Room*），比起《草間彌生的窺探秀》晚了七個月，又再次打擊了草間彌生，但是她並未因此而倒下。草間彌生再次在掌握主流勢力的西方藝術中站穩腳步。這次，她高舉「圓點女祭司」的旗幟，打出「草間，草間，草間－世界第一位執念藝術家」的口號，她強調她的痛苦和病因源自於社會不公的評斷，但是，性別絕對不是用來評鑑藝術好壞的標準。她決定擴大戰場，暫時放下主流藝術圈的恩怨情仇和中產階層的品味，將她的藝術推向廣大的普羅大眾，做群眾會喜愛的藝術，而不是市場所擁抱的那些。她像先知一樣預示了眾人按讚的藝術價值，這也難怪她近年來在世界各地的大小展覽，都受到群眾瘋狂的擁戴，轟動程度是任何當代的藝術家所無法企及的，因為她早就深諳藝術為眾人而藝術的道理。

從表面上看草間彌生1965年開始從事的偶發藝術和表演藝術似乎相當驚世駭俗，但是如果生活在1960年代中期的美國，應該可以理解那時嬉皮文化從美國東岸到西岸都相當普遍，留著長髮，經常衣不蔽體的年輕人，主張愛與和平，反戰而且崇尚自然，身體既是自然的一部分，以身體作為創作的場域，甚至裸體，都並不誇張或突兀。草間彌生巧妙地使用了她的招牌符號「圓點」，紅的、黃的、綠色的圓點代表太陽、月亮和地球，滿布圓點的人體，在草間彌生的眼裡，等於是人體「自我消融」到宇宙自然中的過程，並非刻意挑釁裸體的禁忌。我認為草間彌生當時的創作狀態是時代的大環境提供給她的舞臺和支援，自然發生，自然落幕，但是畢竟西方的文化和她的故鄉日本有很大的差異性，這段藝術生涯對於草間彌生個人的意義，應該是利弊參半的結果。所幸草間彌生在1968年發表的影片《草間的自我消融》（*Kusama's Self-obliterations*），記錄了她前一年的表演，還能夠留給後人對她這一世時期的作品進行更進一步的研究。這部影片在當年發行時，受到美國法規的一些限制，但是影片依然在國際影展頻頻獲得殊榮，獲得比利時第4屆國際短片獎、安娜堡（Ann Arbor）電影節銀獎、第2屆馬里蘭（Maryland）電影節獎。

1969年草間彌生在紐約現代美術館雕塑公園進行的《盛大的狂歡喚醒死者》（*Grand Orgy to Awaken the Dead*）吸引了大量的媒體報導，算是非常地轟動，但畢竟又是一個突擊式的展示活動，直到1998年草間彌生受邀到美國主要的美術館進行巡迴展《永恆的愛：草間彌生，1958-1968》（*Love Forever: Yayoi Kusama, 1958–1968*），也巡展到紐約現代美術館，悠悠三十年過去了，她終於在主流的美術館正式被邀請舉辦個人的回顧展。1970年草間彌生短暫回國後，1970年代初草間彌生經常在歐洲舉辦個展並且進行街頭的偶發表演藝術，也在歐洲許多城市推出她設計的服裝走秀，1972年回到紐約以後開始寫作。然而，打擊再度來臨，草間彌生長期交往的男友，藝術家喬瑟夫・科奈爾（Joseph Cornell）在年底因為心臟病而驟然去世，草間彌生的健康情況也日益惡化，決定返回日本療養。日本大男子主義的藝壇並未有任何改善，她先前在美國的豐功偉業也未必受到保守的日本藝壇的認同，再加上日本居住空間狹窄，使得她無法從事大尺度的創作。藝術，是草間彌生永恆的愛，她不可能停頓下來，這時她轉而從事寫作，陶瓷創作和小幅的水彩、粉彩和拼貼作品。1975年草間彌生自願住進東京地區的療養院，一直到現在不曾離開，幾年後還在附近安排了私人工作室，每天定時往返規律地進行創作。1970年代在日本的草間彌生仍然有國內外零星參展的機會，但是回國後她在藝術圈的活動量，還是遠遠不及她的紐約時期。

轉機發生在1981年，日本國立現代藝術館舉辦《1960年代：日本當代藝術的十年變化》（*The 1960s: A Decade of Change in Contemporary Japanese Art*），草間彌生和其他29位日本重量級的當代藝術家同台展出，奠定她在日本藝壇的學術地位。1983年草間彌生的小說《克裡斯多夫男娼窟》（The Hustler's Grotto of Christopher Street)獲得日本第10屆野性時代新人獎。1984年她獲得惠特尼美國藝術博物館的邀請，參加一項回顧性的重要展覽《砰！普普藝術，極簡主義和表演藝術的爆炸1958-1964》（*Blam! The Explosion of Pop, Minimalism and Performance 1958–1964*），將草間彌生在紐約時期的成就，正式收錄在主流藝壇的認可行列之中。1987年在北九州市立美術館（Kitakyusyu Municipal Museum of Art）舉辦第一次的回顧展。進入1980年代草間彌生再度活躍起來，世界各地的邀約不斷，出版物一本接連一本，她作為代表日本當代藝術的身份在國內也普遍受到肯定，到1993年代表日本在威尼斯雙年展日本國家館以個展形式展出，她的聲望如日中天，之後她的人氣持續攀升，成為國際雙年展、三年展的常客，媒體追捧的明星藝術家，公共藝術作品遍佈全球，圓點南瓜繼圓環成為家喻戶曉的草間彌生符號，草間彌生旋風為她自己，也為日本不斷創造奇蹟式的成功，包括在國際金融風暴的2008年，她在1959年所作的〈無限的網-第2號〉照樣拍出580萬美金（USD$5,800,000）的天價，打破任何女性藝術家的記錄。

草間彌生的藝術事業發跡於上一世紀中期，但是進入西元2000年以後，她完全晉升為一位超越國籍，超越性別，超越年齡的新紀元的超級明星藝術家。2004年她在日本東京森美術館的個展吸引了超過52萬人次的參觀人數，她是國際藝術博覽會最熱門的當代藝術家，大大小小展覽同時在世界幾大洲進行，2011年她和路易威登合作的《路易威登×草間彌生》（*LOUIS VUITTON × YAYOI KUSAMA Collection*）系列，終於實現了她在1960年代擁抱群眾的目標，她不但征服了西方主流藝術的勢力，還讓「圓點女王」的紅髮形象變成無人不知，無人不曉的風雲人物。

我是1973年到美國洛杉磯求學，也差不多就那個時候，草間彌生因病回了日本。那個時代觀念藝術方興未艾，行為藝術盛行，所以草間彌生1960年代在紐約的許多事蹟，大家都耳熟能詳，她是那一代觀念式行為藝術的先鋒，也是極少數亞洲藝術家活躍於紐約（甚至全美國）的罕例，從那時開始，比我年長20餘歲的草間彌生，就是我心目中的偶像。一直到1993年在威尼斯第45屆雙年展，才第一次見到草間彌生本人，當時她代表日本國家館參加威尼斯雙年展，我看到她幾次，她的身邊總圍滿許許多多各國的媒體記者和觀眾，我根本沒有機會靠近她。後來我在臺北和上海策劃的大型國際展，數度跟大田畫廊（Ota Fine Arts）借展草間彌生的作品，總算間接地接觸到草間彌生。因為從上海回到南韓出任大邱市立美術館館長的金善姬（Kim Sumhee）女士，策劃了草間彌生的首次亞洲巡迴展，她出差到東京時，安排了我和草間彌生正式見了面，還一起拍了照。

草間彌生亞洲巡迴展《夢我所夢》的起航，完全因為韓國大邱美術館金善姬館長的緣故，她和草間彌生結識多年，這個展覽作為她受聘為大邱市立美術館館長，送給大邱市民最大的禮物。2013年7月15日大邱市長親臨主持草間彌生《夢我所夢》的開幕，啟動了亞洲巡展的序幕，展覽破天荒地為大邱美術館迎來30餘萬參觀人數，之後巡展到上海當代藝術館，參觀人數照樣突破了30萬。《夢我所夢》大規模展出草間彌生各時期的藝術創作，包括繪畫、裝置和雕塑，尤其2009年開始創作的〈我的永恆靈魂〉（*MY ETERNAL SOUL*）系列，草間彌生更是投注大量心血，至今已創作超過400多件大型油畫作品。還有數件可與觀眾互動的作品，例如〈曼哈頓自殺慣犯之歌〉（*Song of a Manhattan Suicide Addict*），可在鏡屋裡聆聽草間彌生優美的歌聲，更是不容錯過。希望藉由本次的展覽讓更多人看到草間彌生全面且多元的藝術創作脈絡。這次在金善姬館長和草間彌生工作室，大田畫廊的鼎力支援下，終於來到臺灣巡展，由旺旺中時集團時藝多媒體、三立集團闊林文創共同主辦，Future Pass協辦，台新銀行贊助，除春節期間在高雄市立美術館開幕，暑期則在台中的國立臺灣美術館登場，同時，臺北也有相關的教育推廣活動，使得草間彌生到臺灣的第一次大型個展，會是亞洲巡迴展中，規模最大，內容最多元與豐富的。

草間彌生是20至21世紀當代藝術的代表人物，她也是第一位真正名聞四海擁有全球性高知名度的超級明星藝術家，必然是文明史中名垂青史的女大師，她的成就，古往今來都沒有任何其他女性藝術家可以比擬。如今86歲高齡的草間彌生，是當今藝術界的女神，她的神秘人生，已經成了不朽的傳奇。

參觀《夢我所夢》讓我們有幸福的感覺，允許我們進入草間彌生的奇幻世界，得以一探她那引人入勝的無限時空。藝術，是她永恆的愛，也是她給予世人最珍貴的禮物。

---

[1] 唐納德・賈德《藝術新聞》，1959年10月。

[2] 草間彌生《無限的網》，2011年。

An Art Life of a Dream Kusama Dreamed

Victoria Lu

It was to a prosperous merchant family in the city of Matsumoto that Kusama Yayoi was born on March 22, 1929. It was a developing and growing society in the Nagano Prefecture of Japan, but due to her parents' untrusting marriage, Kusama led an unusual childhood,struggling from dis communication with her mother. She has experienced frequent hallucinationssince childhood. Along with having to suffer her mother's obsessive, irrational treatment, she even considered suicide. Painting was Kusama Yayoi's salvation, and a means of escape through her boundless imagination. At that time Kusama drew a portrait of her mother, filling in the entire picture with dots of different sizes. In the future, these dots would become her artistic symbol and personal emblem. After graduating from Matsumoto First Girl's High School, Kusama Yayoi entered Kyoto Municipal School of Arts and Crafts, where she majored in Japanese painting. This experience gave her basic training in painting techniques.

Kusama Yayoi had already begun displaying her artistic genius at a young age and in 1949, at the age of 20, her painting *Lingering Dream* was selected for the Second Creative Arts Exhibition. Unfortunately her relationship with her mother failed to improve, and her mother could not understand or appreciate her daughter's unique artistic talent, advising against and even attempting to block her daughter's pursuit of art. Kusama Yayoi sought expansion and acceptance, but this was only one of the reasons she felt the urge to go oversees. It was extremely bold and forward-looking thinking for a Japanese woman of those times, and only the beginning of a lifetime of making us all rethink social norms.

It's important to see how Kusama's art was a natural response to the visceral world around her. She seemed unaffected by the environment around her and cared very little for prevailing artistic trends or styles. Kusama's creativity is based on her artistic sense and her own unique experiences. She described such experience as follows:"One day I was looking at the red flower patterns of the tablecloth on a table, and when I looked up I saw the same pattern covering the ceiling, the windows and the walls, and finally all over the room, my body and the universe. I felt as if I had begun to self-obliterate, to revolve in the infinity of endless time and the absoluteness of space, and be reduced to nothingness. As I realized it was actually happening and not just in my imagination, I was frightened. I knew I had to run away lest I should be deprived of my life by the spell of the red flowers. I ran desperately up the stairs. The steps below me began to fall apart and I fell down the stairs straining my ankle." Kusama Yayoi's concept of "self-obliteration" was obviously already taking shape at this time, and would subsequently become a deep-seated part of her creative thinking.

Finally determined to leave Japan, Kusama Yayoi wrote a letter to French President at that time in which she expressed her wish to go to France. To her surprise she received a response, which informed her that she must go to the French embassy and apply for a cultural interchange program, which included a French language test. Kusama started to study French, and even got a place in an art school in Paris, however preparing for a few solo shows at the same time in Tokyo forced her to postpone her travels to France. Shortly afterwards she saw an album of the paintings of Georgia O'Keeffe in a used bookstore, and discovered that O'Keeffe was a famous American artist. In order to send a letter to her, Kusama rode a train for six hours to visit the American embassy in Tokyo, where she found a way to contact O'Keeffe through a copy of Who's Who. This was the start of Kusama's communication with Georgia O'Keeffe, and was the real step in her persistent plans to go overseas.

Before going to the US, Kusama Yayoi burned hundreds of her art works at the bank of her local river. She was determined to leave Japan and showed her will for new creative achievement in an unknown land. She obtained an invitation from Zoe Dusanne Gallery in 1957, a prestigious modern art gallery in Seattle at the time, and arranged to hold a solo exhibition there. Kusama Yayoi finally got her opportunity and flew off to the United States. By that time, Alfred Stieglitz had already passed away, and Georgia O'Keeffe had moved to New Mexico. O'Keeffe was still able to write a letter of recommendation for Kusama, and even later made a special trip to meet Kusama. After her exhibition in Seattle, Kusama moved to New York in 1958. Her life after first arriving in New York was extremely grim, spending her first winter hungry, cold, and often in poor health, with only the slightest hope of earning a living. In these harsh conditions, painting remained her key means of redemption as she created her large-scale Infinity Nets paintings–now considered among her classic works—during this time.

In 1959, Donald Judd, an artist and an art critic for ARTnews, after viewing *Infinity Nets*, noted that "the effect is both complex and simple... Essentially it is produced by the interaction of the two close somewhat parallel planes … at points merging at the surface plane and at others diverging slightly but powerfully." [1]

When commenting on her own work, Kusama Yayoi describes it as "dissolution and accumulation; propagation and separation; particulate obliteration and unseen reverberations from the universe. - these were to become the foundations of my art and they were already taking shape at this time" [2]

In the wake of World War II, New York replaced Paris as the world's art center, giving rise to abstract expressionism and the emergence of pop art. Kusama Yayoi was one of a very small number of female Asian artists working in the New York area, and she quickly received attention. Her mental condition allowed her to concentrate exclusively on whatever she was doing, making it so that she could work for 40 or 50 hours at a stretch without resting or sleeping. She was also fearless, with the ability to call on several hundred people to take part under her command in grand performance art. She even dared to write an open letter to President Nixon proclaiming her anti-war stance and requesting that the president immediately terminate the Vietnam War. She did things her own way. As a result, all of her art exudes a primordial appeal and the power or originality. While her monochrome *Infinity Nets* paintings appear to be minimalist works, she produced them before the minimalist movement had gotten underway. Her installation works employing multiple images were made before Andy Warhol did anything similar. And her sewn phallic installations came before Claes Oldenburg's soft sculptures. She freely chooses to use whatever media she wants in her work, including the body, and her artistic form remains totally unconstrained. Her work has spanned the range of paintings, sculpture, installation art, performance art, photography, film, video, clothing design, text, and almost any kind of artistic form that can be imagined.

Looking back on her artistic development from the late 1950s through her New York period, we can see Kusama Yayoi was always an unrestrained natural pioneer. While her 1960s installation works and performance art typically expressed a strong feminist consciousness, she had absolutely no relationship with the 1970's American feminist movement, as her work was produced well before even the emergence of that movement. Her feminist tendencies were expressed solely as the reflection of her life in her work, and derived exclusively from her experience as a woman. Like some of the greatest artists in history, she magically transformed her life into her art.

In New York, Kusama Yayoi's creative energies were in full blaze during the 1960s, and she occupied her own territory at the front line of contemporary art. With her obsessive-compulsive disorder adding to her natural artistic talent, her creativity and productivity surpassed that of most individuals. Hoping to make a name for herself in New York, which would let her bring her reputation back to Japan with her, she embarked on an all-round assault on the art world. The output and sheer diversity of her work were simply incredible, as she incontestably stood head and shoulders above other Asian artists of the time.

She had already been invited to participate in some group exhibitions in 1959, and had held solo exhibitions. When she was invited to participate in the major international exhibition "Monochrome Malerei" ("Monochrome Paintings") at Germany's Städtisches Museum in 1960, she and Mark Rothko were the only two artists invited from New York. At that time, Kusama Yayoi's works were displayed together with those of such heavyweight European avant garde artists as Lucio Fontana, Yves Klein, Piero Manzoni, and Günther Uecker. During the following year, she was invited to participate in the "1961 Whitney Annual" at New York's Whitney Museum. These achievements far surpassed those of any other Asian artists of the time. Even more incredible was that the art critic Donald Judd, who would later declare that "painting is dead," bought one of Kusama Yayoi's *Infinity Nets* paintings in installments; later the two also became friends after Kusama moved into his apartment building. When Kusama Yayoi was making soft sculptures, Judd often helped her and encouraged her.

In June 1962, Kusama Yayoi was invited to display her soft sculpture series *Accumulation* for the first time at a group exhibition held at New York's Green Gallery. Other participants at this exhibition, which was later acclaimed as the first exhibition of pop art, included Claes Oldenburg, James Rosenquist, George Segal, and Andy Warhol. Claes Oldenburg displayed only a set of processed suits at this exhibition, while Kusama Yayoi exhibited a sofa and seat decorated with sewn phalluses, which caused viewers to marvel. Claes Oldenburg cannot have failed to observe this; during the fall of the same year, he held a solo exhibition in which he raised the banner of soft sculpture, which immediately earned him an international reputation. He nevertheless denied that Kusama had inspired him. To Kusama's disappointment, the Green Gallery went on to sign a contract with Oldenburg instead of her. This incident was one of the major factors that caused a recurrence of her mental illness. In her hermetically sealed personal environment, Kusama Yayoi's creativity never ceased, and she completed her Aggregation: One Thousand Boat Show in 1963. This large room installation, which displayed her soft sculpture and multiple images, seemed to explain everything.

Kusama Yayoi has claimed to be the first "obsessional artist." She was afraid of men and sex, which in fact prompted her to produce sprawling phallic images and objects. From the planar paintings in *Infinity Nets*, her works increasingly spread out into space, overcoming restrictions imposed by space and media. She also employed ready-made objects, photographs, and pictures in the soft sculptures that she produced in large quantities. Her installations bore witness to her new explosion of creativity, and she started making use of the endless reflections of mirrors to truly extend *Infinity Nets* to the boundlessness of space. Her 1965 *Infinity Mirror Room - Phalli's Field "Floor Show"* and 1966 *Kusama's Peep Show* showed that she had perfected the use of reflections from mirrors as an artistic technique, and the mirror room installation became another symbol of Kusama's art.

In 1966, Kusama Yayoi used self-deprecating "surprise attack" methods to participate in the 33rd Venice Biennale, where she displayed her Narcissus Garden. In this work, she placed 1,500 mirror balls on two patches of grass in front of the Italian pavilion. She then donned a gorgeous kimono, and began selling her mirror balls for 1,200 lira (approximately US$2) each in the name of "Your Narcissus." This immediately attracted the notice of the Biennale's organizing committee, who promptly prohibited her from selling the balls at the Biennale. This unsettling decision was finally readdressed 27 years later, when Kusama returned to the Biennale with great fanfare. This time, she displayed a large installation consisting of a room filled with mirrors, in which black dots on a yellow background were endlessly reflected. She then appeared at the event wearing a specially-made form-fitting long gown featuring black dots on a yellow background, as well as a tall, pointed hat bearing the same design. The attention attracted by Kusama was off the chart, while she even personally stood in the doorway greeting visitors, and giving out small pumpkins. Visitors formed a long line outside the Japan pavilion, as she was unquestionably the star artist of that year's show.

In spite of her successes, Kusama Yayoi's nightmares still followed her like a dark shadow. In October of 1966, Lucas Samaras displayed his *Mirror Room* at a major gallery in New York only seven months after Kusama's Peep Show. This became another distress for Kusama, but she did not admit defeat because of it. Kusama's response to the Western art community which at that time was controlled by a group of powerful men was again a major surprise. This "Polka-dot Priestess" tossed out the slogan "Kusama, Kusama, Kusama – The World's First Obsessional Artist,". She emphasized that while her suffering and illness had originated from society's unfair judgments, it was absolutely impermissible to use gender as a standard for assessing the quality of art. She decided to expand the scope of her fight, and turned her back on the mainstream art circles and their bourgeois tastes. She instead reached out artistically to the masses, and started making art that appealed to the general public, rather than the art market at that time. Like a prophet, she pointed the way to artistic values that the public could sympathize with. No wonder her various exhibitions held around the world in recent years have earned her fanatic public support, while her work causes a sensation that no other contemporary artist can match. This is all because of her early realization that art for the masses is true art.

While Kusama Yayoi's early involvement in happenings and performance art starting in 1965 seems rather remarkable from today's perspective, it should be remembered that hippy culture had spread across much of the United States by the mid-1960s, and young people wearing long hair and shabby clothing were proclaiming love, peace, and an end to the war. Since many people were expressing a newfound reverence for nature, and the body was certainly a part of nature, the use of the body as a creative setting, even when nude, was nothing extreme or unexpected. For Kusama Yayoi, covering her body with polka dots was equivalent to the process of self-obliteration of the body to the nature of the universe, and was not deliberate defiance of the taboo against nudity. I feel that Kusama Yayoi's creative state at the time was something that occurred naturally and ended naturally on the stage provided by the environment as a whole at that time. However, great cultural differences remained between the West and her homeland of Japan, and as a consequence, this stage in her art career had roughly equal positive and negative significance to her as an individual. Her 1968 film *Kusama's Self Obliterations*, which records her performances during the previous year is available for those who wish to further research her works from this era. This film won numerous awards at international film festivals including the 4th International Short Feature Award in Belgium, a silver medal at the Ann Arbor Film Festival, and the 2nd Maryland Film Festival Award.

In 1969, Kusama Yayoi conducted her performance art project *Grand Orgy to Awaken the Dead* in the Sculpture Garden of the New York Museum of Modern Art, which caused a sensation and attracted extensive media coverage. However, this was really just another surprise attack style art activity. In 1998, when Kusama Yayoi was invited to bring her touring exhibition "Love Forever: Yayoi Kusama, 1958–1968" to major museums of fine art in the United States, the exhibition made a stop at the New York Museum of Modern Art. At that time, after 30 years, she was finally invited to hold an individual retrospective exhibition at this mainstream museum of fine art. After a brief return to Japan in 1970, Kusama spent a lot of her early 70's holding solo exhibitions and happenings in Europe, and she also introduced clothing she had designed at fashion shows in many European cities. After returning to New York in 1972, her long-time boyfriend Joseph Cornell passed away suddenly due to heart disease. Soon after Kusama's health began to deteriorate and she decided to return to Japan to recuperate. Arriving in Japan, Kusama found that the male chauvinism prevailing in Japan's art community had not improved, and her amazing achievements in the United States did not necessarily give her much credit with more conservative Japanese artists. In addition, the cramped living conditions in Japan prevented her from creating art on a large scale. Art nevertheless remained Kusama's eternal love, and she found it impossible to stop making art. At this time, she turned her attention to writing, ceramics, watercolors, pastels, and collages. In 1975, Kusama Yayoi voluntarily moved into a mental institute in Tokyo, and has remained a resident there until the present. During the subsequent years she went to make art at her studio, which she acquired near her hospital, every day at the same time and maintained very regular working habits. Throughout the 1970s, Kusama continued to sporadically hold domestic and foreign exhibitions, but her level of activity in art circles remained far below that of her time in New York.

A turn for the better occurred in 1981, when the National Museum of Modern Art, Tokyo held "The 1960s: A Decade of Change in Contemporary Japanese Art", which contained works from Kusama Yayoi and 29 other heavyweight Japanese contemporary artists.This exhibition proved her academic status in Japan's art community. In 1983, Kusama Yayoi's novel *The Hustler's Grotto of Christopher Street* won Yasei Jidai magazine's 10th Literary Award for New Writers. In 1984, she was invited by the Whitney Museum to participate in the major retrospective exhibition "Blam! The Explosion of Pop, Minimalism and Performance 1958–1964," which formally granted Kusama Yayoi's achievements during her New York the imprimatur of the mainstream art community. In 1987, her first ever retrospective exhibition was held at the Kitakyusyu Municipal Museum of Art. Increasing her level of activity during the 1980s, Kusama responding to a stream of invitations from around the world, and published book after book. At home, she received widespread recognition as Japan's leading exponent of contemporary art, and in 1993 represented Japan with a solo exhibition in the Japanese pavilion at the Venice Biennale. Her reputation soared, her popular appeal continued to climb, and she made regular appearances at international biennial and triennial exhibitions. She assumed the role of a star artist pursued by the media, and her works were installed as public art around the world. Dotted Pumpkin became one of her best-known symbols. The Kusama Yayoi whirlwind created miraculous success for her and for Japan. For instance, in 2008, during the international financial crisis, her 1959 *Infinity Nets-No. 2* still fetched the typically colossal price of US$5.8 million, which broke the previous record for a work by a female artist.

While Kusama Yayoi's artistic career got underway during the middle of the previous century, after 2000 she has been promoted as a new-age superstar artist transcending nationality, gender, and age. A solo exhibition at Tokyo's Mori Art Museum in 2004 attracted more than 520,000 viewers. She is a hot commodity at international art festivals, and her large and small exhibitions are constantly being held on all five major continents. In 2011, she collaborated with Louis Vuitton in the form of the "Louis Vuitton × Yayoi Kusama Collection" series. She has finally achieved the goals of her 1960s embrace of popular art; not only has she conquered the heights of Western mainstream art, but she has also made herself—in the form of the "Polka Dot Queen"—an icon of popular culture now known to all.

When I came to Los Angeles to attend university in 1973, Kusama was already returning to Japan due to poor health. Conceptual art was still ascendant in those days, and performance art still flourishing, with Kusama's 1960s achievements in New York still fresh and familiar. She had been in the vanguard of the generation of conceptual performance art, and was one of an extremely small number of Asian artists who were active in New York (or anywhere in the United States). From that moment, Kusama Yayoi, who is more than 20 years my senior, became my idol. I saw her in person for the first time in 1993 at the 45th Venice Biennale, where she was participating as a representative of Japan. Each time I saw her, she was surrounded by a gaggle of reporters and viewers from many countries, and I never got the opportunity to get close to her. Subsequently on several occasions, when curating major international exhibitions in Taipei and Shanghai, I was able to borrow her works from the Ota Fine Arts Gallery. This was perhaps my way of indirectly coming in contact with her. And like serendipity, Kim Sunhee, who returned from Shanghai to South Korea to serve as director of the Daegu Art Museum, arranged for me to formally meet with Kusama Yayoi, and have my photo taken with her, when she was in Tokyo arranging Kusama Yayoi's first Asian touring exhibition.

That Kusama Yayoi's Asian touring exhibition "A Dream I Dreamed" first became a reality was completely due to the efforts of Director Kim Sunhee of Korea's Daegu Art Museum. She has known Kusama Yayoi for many years, and this exhibition represents the greatest gift to the residents of Daegu since she was made director of the Daegu Art Museum. On July 15, 2013, the mayor of Daegu personally hosted the opening ceremony for "A Dream I Dreamed" exhibition, which kicked off the exhibition's Asian tour. The exhibition achieved unprecedented attendance of over 300,000 visitors at the Daegu Art Museum, and was subsequently held at the Museum of Contemporary Art Shanghai, where it also attracted more than 300,000 visitors. "A Dream I Dreamed" is one of the biggest scale exhibitions of Kusama which mainly focuses on Kusama's recent works including painting, installations and sculptures. The highlight is the colorful paintings from the "My Eternal Soul" series, which Kusama is currently putting her heart and soul in. Kusama started to execute this series in 2009 and it has now grown into her biggest series counting over 400 large scale canvases. The exhibition is indeed a special opportunity for the Asian citizens to see Kusama's very latest creativity. There are also a good number of installations that are able to interact with viewers including "Song of a Manhattan Suicide Addict", a mirror installation with Kusama singing.

Thanks to support from Director Kim Sunhee, KUSAMA Enterprise, and the Ota Fine Arts, this exhibition has finally arrived in Taiwan, where it has been organized by Media Sphere Communication Ltd., Want Want China Times Media Group and Greenland Creative Co., Ltd., co-organized by New Face Inc., and sponsored by Taishin Bank. It had be held at the Kaohsiung Museum of Fine Arts—its first stop in Taiwan—during the New Year's Holiday, and will then proceed to the National Taiwan Museum of Fine Arts in Taichung. As a result, we can look forward to Kusama Yayoi's first major solo exhibition in Taiwan being the largest and most diverse exhibition of her Asian tour.

Kusama Yayoi is one of the most representative contemporary artists of the 20th and 21st centuries, and is the first true superstar artists with global recognition. History will regard her as a preeminent female master. Her achievements are unmatched by any other female artist, of the past or the future. Today, at the advanced age of 86, Kusama Yayoi is a goddess of the art world, and her mysteriousness has become a lasting legend.

Viewing" *A Dream I Dreamed"* has given us a feeling of being blessed. It has permitted us to enter Kusama Yayoi's fantastic world, and given us a glimpse of her boundless, enchanted universe. Art is her eternal love, and is her priceless gift to the people of the world.

---

1. Donald Judd, *Art News*, October 1959

2. Yayoi Kusama, *Infinity Net*, 2011

まぼろクラ　我所夢

生之祈望

草間彌生

從光芒萬丈的天空中，

悄然浮現我對真理的無限渴望，

從宇宙的盡頭，他們終舊降臨，

與死者和生者言談，

我心滿溢情感，

此刻，打自心底，我啟口，

淚水盈眶，

在這目不暇給的人世間，

充滿了閃爍的愛與希望，

曾經如此支撐著我。

我心低回，

來自宇宙盡頭，

那深沉的愛、恨、悲傷與絕望，

在這些夾縫中，

在人們盎然的情愛、歡慶與人道之愛中間，

我累蓄了生之祈望。

陷身於如此的絕望之間，

我懷疑明日我是否依然健在？

是要我每天都捫心自問那答案嗎？

時不時以我的至誠。

生きていきたいのに

草間弥生

光かがやいた空の中より
わたしの求道への限りもなく
心をこめた望みが、しずかに
やってくる。たった今、それ達は
宇宙の果てより、いよいよ
死んだ人々や生きている人々に問いかけてきたのだ。
心を一杯にみたして
わたしはいま心の底から
溢れ出る涙をもって言う
人の世のめくるめく
かがやいた愛と希望に充ちてわたしをささえた
大いなる生への願望と
愛に充ちた宇宙の果てまでも
とどろく心の限りの
愛とにくしみ、そして悲しみと失望のはざまの中で、
わたしは今日もまた
たくさんの人間愛と
人生への賛美と敬愛のはざまで、生きてゆく事への
希望をつみかさねて、この失望のただ中で
明日もまた、生きてゆけるのだろうか。
わたしの心に毎日聞いてみようか。
時の間に間に、心をこめて。

I Want to Keep on Living, But........ .

Yayoi Kusama

From within the radiantly shining sky,
appear quietly my infinitely earnest wishes for
finding the truth.
From the end of the universe, they have finally come out
to talk to the dead and the living.
With my heart filled with emotions,
I say now from the bottom of my heart
with tears welled up in my eyes.
A wish for a great life that has supported me
in this dizzying world of people filled with glittering love and hope.
And a deep sense of love and hate, and of sorrow and despair
that reverberates through the end of the universe.
Placed in between these, and between abundant human love,
and celebration and love of humanity,
I accumulate hopes for a living.
In the midst of this despair,
I wonder if I can still live tomorrow.
Shall I ask my heart everyday for an answer.
From time to time, and with utmost sincerity.

圓點執念
複合媒材
尺寸可變
2015

Dots Obsession
mixed mediat
dimension variable
2015

為摯愛的鬱金香永恆祈禱

金屬、玻璃纖維
聚氨酯塗料、貼紙
201x170xH295cm
181x170xH235cm
210x170xH229.5cm
2013

With All My Love for the Tulips, I Pray Forever

metal, F.R.P.
urethane paint, stickers
201x170xH295cm
181x170xH235cm
210x170xH229.5cm
2013

自戀庭園
不鏽鋼球
1,500顆 (φ30cm)
1966/2015

Narcissus Garden
stainless steel sphere
1,500spheres(φ30cm)
1966/2015

我在這裡，但什麼也不是
乙烯貼紙、紫外線螢光燈、傢俱、居家用品
尺寸可變
2015

I'm Here, but Nothing
vinyl stickers, ultraviolet fluorescent lights,
furniture, household objects
dimensions variable
2015

小正 / SHO-CHAN

小童 / TOKO-CHAN

小龍 / TATCHAN

小歐 / OHCHAN

小次郎 / JIRO-CHAN

小健二 / KENJI-CHAN

小正 / 小歐
玻璃纖維、聚氨酯塗料
28x88xH68cm
2013

SHO-CHAN / OHCHAN
F.R.P.(Fiberglass Reinforced Plastic),
urethane paint
28x88xH68cm
2013

小童 / 小次郎
玻璃纖維、聚氨酯塗料
48x101xH80cm
2013

TOKO-CHAN / JIRO-CHAN
F.R.P.(Fiberglass Reinforced Plastic),
urethane paint
48x101xH80cm
2013

小龍 / 小健二
玻璃纖維、聚氨酯塗料
60x134xH94cm
2013

TATCHAN / KENJI-CHAN
F.R.P.(Fiberglass Reinforced Plastic),
urethane paint
60x134xH94cm
2013

Collaboration between Yayoi Kusama and Queensland Art Gallery.
Commissioned Queensland Art Gallery. Gift of the artist through the
Queensland Art Gallery Foundation 2012.

消融之屋
傢俱、白色油漆、圓點貼紙

尺寸可變
2002-2015

The Obliteration Room
furniture, white paint, dot stickers
dimensions variable
2002-2015

57

無限鏡屋-靈魂閃耀
鏡面、木板、LED燈
金屬、壓克力板、水
415x415xH 287.4cm
2014

Infinity Mirrored Room -
Brilliance of the Souls

mirror, wooden panel, LED,
metal, acrylic panel, water
415x415xH 287.4cm
2014

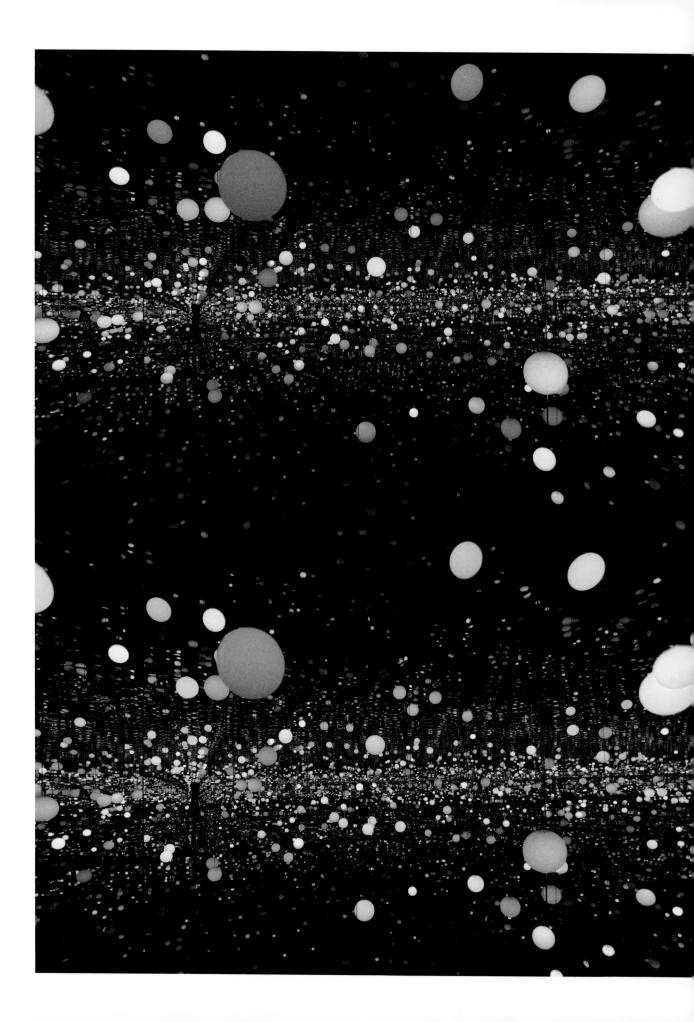

無限鏡屋-永恆的愛
鏡子、金屬、電燈泡、木
210x205xH240cm
1994

Infinity Mirrored Room-
Love Forever
mirror, metal, electric bulb, wood
210x205xH240cm
1994

重複視覺，陽具之舟
填充縫製合成布料、
發泡橡膠與塑膠、海報
船體：330x145xH70cm
槳：每件200cm

2000

Repetitive-Vision, Phallus-Boat
stuffed sewn synthetic fabric,
foam rubber and plastic, posters
boat:330x145xH70cm,
oars:each 200cm

2000

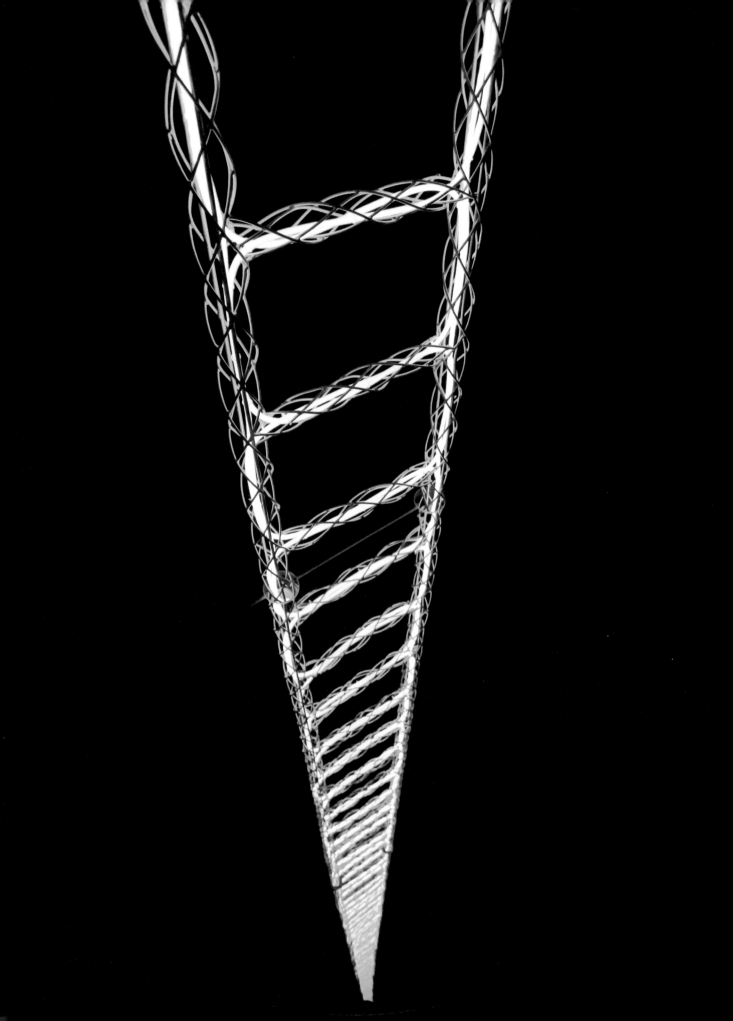

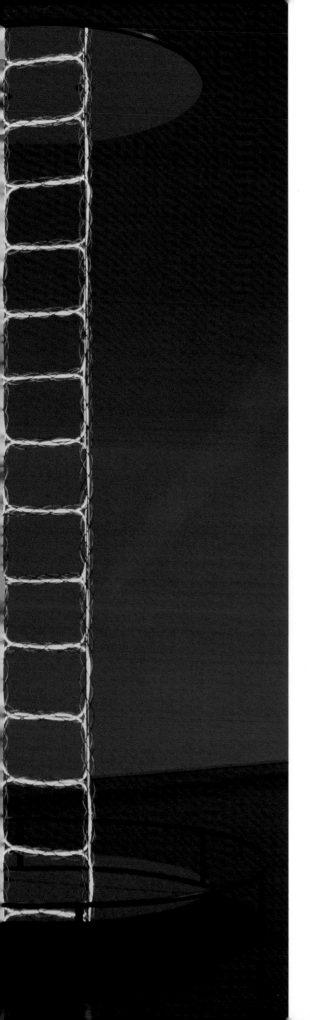

天國之梯
鏡面、金屬、燈、纖維繩
dia.150xH360cm
2012

Ladder to Heaven
mirror,metal, lamp, fibercable
dia.150xH360cm
2012

再生時刻
縫製布料、聚氯胺泡棉
壓克力、木
55件
尺寸可變
2004

The Moment of Regeneration
sewn fabric, urethane foam, acrylic, wood
55 pieces
dimension variable
2004

「曼哈頓自殺慣犯」之歌

草間彌生

服下抗憂鬱劑它便離我而去

錯覺的大門被轟然擊碎

在花的痛苦裡

此刻永不終結

在天國的階梯前

我心在它的慈愛裡將息

空中傳來呼喚

毫無疑問的

一碧如洗

挾著幻想的陰翳

如積雨雲一般堆積

伴著淚水的聲音

吞食堇花的色彩

我化作磐石

不在永恆的如斯

而在即逝的瞬間

「マンハッタン自殺未遂常習犯」の歌

草間弥生

抗鬱剤のんで去ってしまう
錯角の扉撃ち破る
花の煩悶のなかいまは果てなく
天国への階段優雅さに胸果ててしまう
呼んでいるきっと孤空の碧さ透けて
幻覚の影抱擁きわきあがる雲の色
芙蓉いろ食べてみて散るなみだの音

わたしは石になってしまう
時永遠でなく　自殺てる　現在は

Song of a "Manhattan Suicide Addict"

Yayoi Kusama

Swallow antidepressants and it will be gone
Tear down the gate if hallucinations
Amidst the agony of flowers, the present never ends
At the stairs to heaven, my heart expires in their tenderness
Calling from the sky, doubtless, transparent in its shade of blue
Embraced with the shadow of illusion Cumulonimbi arise
Sounds of tears, shed upon eating the colour of cotton rose
I become a stone
Not in time eternal
But in the present that transpires

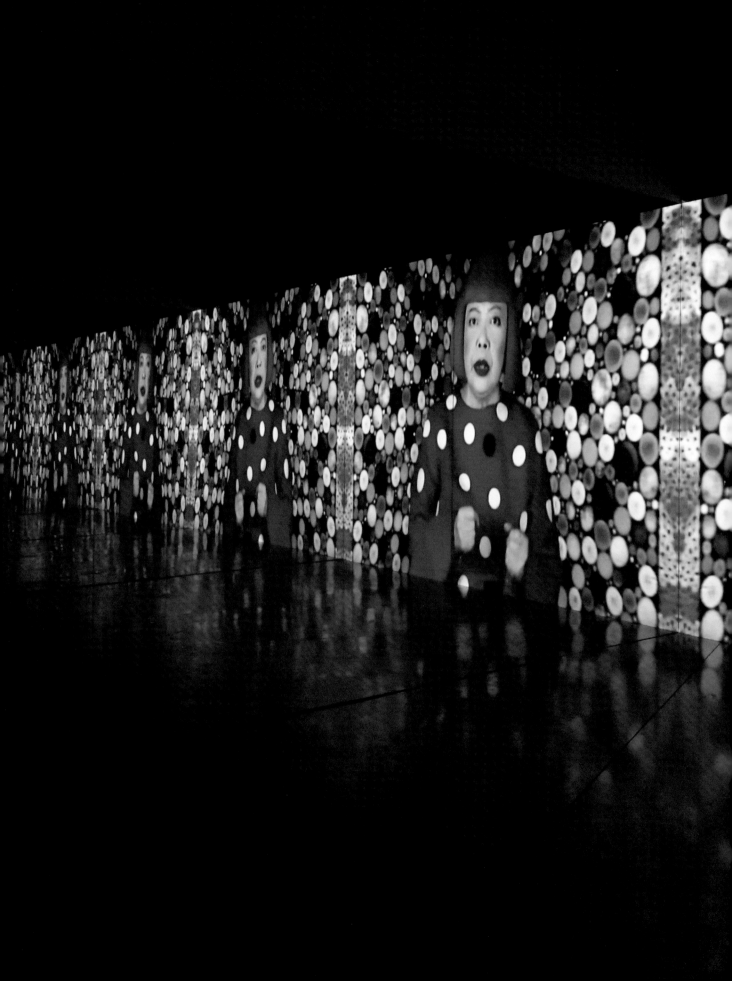

曼哈頓自殺慣犯之歌
錄像（1分24秒）
尺寸可變
2010

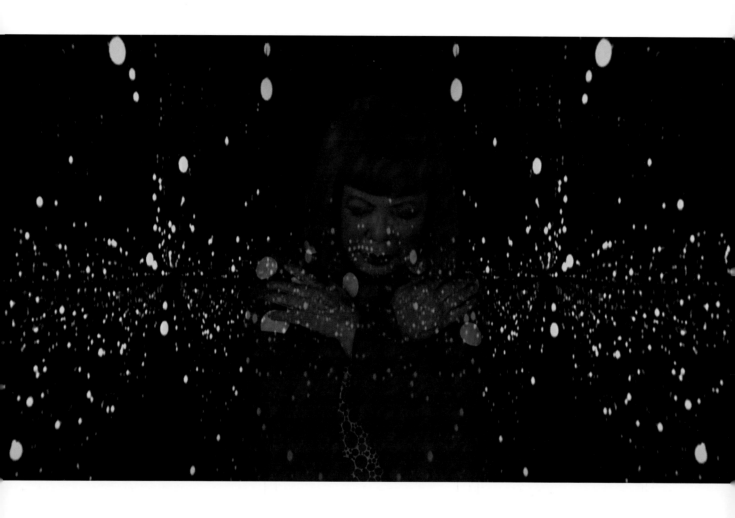

Song of a Manhattan Suicide Addict
video(1min.24 sec.)
dimensions variable
2010

關於南瓜

草間彌生

南瓜，你如此甜美，

你用充滿野性而又幽默的氛圍，

攫住人們的心不放，

是這樣美妙！

我，摯愛南瓜。

南瓜之於我，

幼年起便是心靈之故鄉。

你攜帶著無限大的精神力量，

為全世界人類齊聲歌頌和平與人性做貢獻，

使我心得安寧。

南瓜之於我，

為我心帶來詩一般的平和。

南瓜向我訴說。

南瓜、南瓜、南瓜，

你拿走我心中神聖的願景，

成為支撐世界上全人類生存的

生之歡喜的根源。

南瓜，我為你而活！

「南瓜について」

草間弥生

南瓜は愛嬌があって
すばらしく野性的でユーモラスの雰囲気が
人々の心をとらえてやまない。
わたし、南瓜大好きなの
南瓜は私にとって幼い頃より心の故郷として
無限大の精神性をたずさえて
世界中の人類たちの平和と人間賛美に寄与して
心を安らかにしてくれるのだ。
南瓜は私にとって心の中の
詩的な平和をもたらしてくる。
南瓜は語りかけてくれるのだ。
南瓜、南瓜、南瓜、
わたしの心の神聖な佇まいをもって
世界の全人類が生きている生への歓喜の根元なのだ
南瓜のために私は生き抜いているのだ。

On Pumpkins

Yayoi Kusama

Pumpkins are lovable and their
wonderfully wild and humorous atmosphere
never ceases to capture the hearts of people.
I adore pumpkins.
As my spiritual home since childhood,
and with their infinite spirituality,
they contribute to the peace of mankind across the world
and to the celebration of humanity. And by doing so,
they make me feel at peace.
Pumpkins bring about poetic peace in my mind.
Pumpkins talk to me.
Pumpkins, pumpkins, pumpkins.
Giving off an aura of my sacred mental state,
they embody a base for the joy of living,
a living shared by all of humankind on the earth.
It is for the pumpkins that I keep on going.

大南瓜 / 南瓜 / 南瓜
玻璃纖維、聚氨酯塗料、金屬
φ260xH250cm / φ200xH205cm / φ130xH125cm
2014 / 2013 / 2013

Great Gigantic Pumpkin / Pumpkin / Pumpkin
F.R.P.(FiberglassReinforced Plastic), urethane paint, metal
φ260xH250cm / φ200xH205cm / φ130xH125cm
2014 / 2013 / 2013

奮戰過後，我想在宇宙盡頭死去

草間彌生

愛是永恆！
我曾對著所有人這樣呼喊；
並無休止地為生而煩惱，
不知疲倦地搖晃藝術的求道大旗。
出生至今，
我一路狂奔，從不停歇。
我在名叫世界的舞台上大顯身手，
幾度昨日之衣換新衣，幾番蛻變，
只為創造龐大的作品群。
我的這段「路程」，
在深夜的燈下，
在多少個不眠夜，
無聲激勵著我。
而我，願為世人喚來更多的愛，
留為印記。
我衷心祈願，
世界能夠跨越紛爭、戰爭、恐怖事件與貧富有別的
泥沼；
我願人人和平度日。
我的祈願永不絕衰！
我願借藝術之心的瑰寶－求道石杖，
服務人們，貢獻社會。
路盡頭，我終將老去，
攀登宇宙無比寬闊的天國階梯，
在白雲靜靜鋪展的褥墊上，
我將離開自我；
在湛藍湛藍的天空之褥上，
我將從容地安眠吧？
然後再向地球說再見。

戦いのあとで宇宙の果てで死にたい

草間弥生

すべての人々に愛はとこしえと叫びつづけてきたわたし
そしていつも生きることに悩みつづけ
芸術の求道の旗をふりつづけてきた。
生まれいでてからこのかたそして
今迄走りつづけてきたのだった。
世界という檜舞台でのいくたびかの
昨日の衣を常に新しい衣に脱皮しながら
膨大な作品群を造りつづけてきた
このわたしの「道程」は、真夜中の灯の下で
ねむれぬ幾夜中のしじまに励ましてくれる
そしてもっともっと愛を世に叫び刻印を残したい。
世界の争いや戦争やテロや貧富の泥沼をのりこえることを
心から願って止まない。
人々が平和でくらせるようにと
わたしの願いはつきることもない。
芸術の力をもって斗っていきたいのだ。
芸術の心のかぎりの求道のいしづえをもって
人々に仕え社会に貢献したい。
そのゆきつく先は、わたしはやがて老いて
宇宙の広々とした天国の階段をのぼりつめて、
白雲が静かにつづくしとねで
わたしは自我をはなれ
深々とした青い空のしとねで、
ゆったりとねむりつづけるだろう。
そして地球にサヨナラを伝えるのだ。

After the Battle,
I Want to Die at the End of the Universe

Yayoi Kusama

I who have been shouting Love Forever to all the people.
Having always been distressed over how to live
I have kept carrying the banner for pursuit of art.
And since the time I was born
I have continued running.
On the world stage, constantly shedding my yesterday's clothes for
new ones
I have kept creating an enormous body of work.
This "journey" of mine, under the midnight lamp and
in the stillness of many sleepless nights, has been a source of encour-
agement for me.
I want to shout love louder to the world and to leave my mark there.
To overcome conflicts, wars, terrors, and a morass of rich and poor in
the world,
that is my earnest wish.
May people live in peace I never stop praying for that.
I want to keep fighting with the power of art.
With the pursuit of art as a cornerstone
I want to serve the people and contribute to society.
I will eventually grow old,
walk up a ladder all the way up to heaven in the vast universe.
In a bed of quietly floating white clouds
I depart from myself.
In a bed of deep and blue sky,
I will keep sleeping in comfort.
And I say farewell to the Earth.

我的永恆靈魂
MY ETERNAL SOUL

想要將我所有的愛，
以及夜晚的夢都吃下去
壓克力、畫布
130.3x162cm
2009

ALL ABOUT MY LOVE,
AND I LONG TO EAT A DREAM OF THE NIGHT
acrylic on canvas
130.3x162cm
2009

花季邂逅
壓克力、畫布
130.3x162cm
2009

AN ENCOUNTER WITH
A FLOWERING SEASON
acrylic on canvas
130.3x162cm
2009

遠在宇宙之外追求真理的閃亮之星黯淡無光，
我越探尋真理，它們越璀璨

壓克力、畫布
130.3x162cm
2009

SHINING STARS IN PURSUIT OF THE TRUTH
ARE OFF IN THE DISTANCE BEYOND UNIVERSE,
THE MORE I SOUGHT THE TRUTH,
BRIGHTER THEY SHONE

acrylic on canvas
130.3x162cm
2009

愛帶著宇宙故事來到地球
壓克力、畫布
130.3x162cm
2009

LOVE ARRIVES AT THE EARTH CARRYING
WITH IT A TALE OF THE COSMOS
acrylic on canvas
130.3x162cm
2009

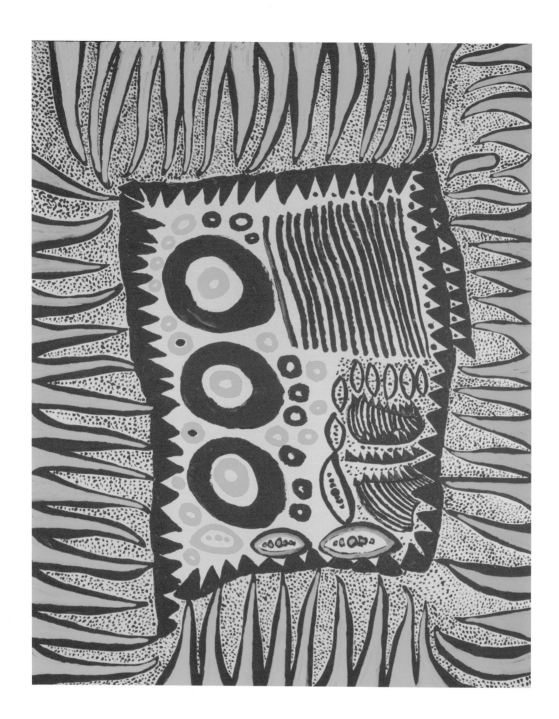

綻放
壓克力、畫布
162x130.3cm
2012

FLOWERING
acrylic on canvas
162x130.3cm
2012

在花園中入眠
壓克力、畫布
162x130.3cm
2011

SLEEPING IN A FLOWER GARDEN
acrylic on canvas
162x130.3cm
2011

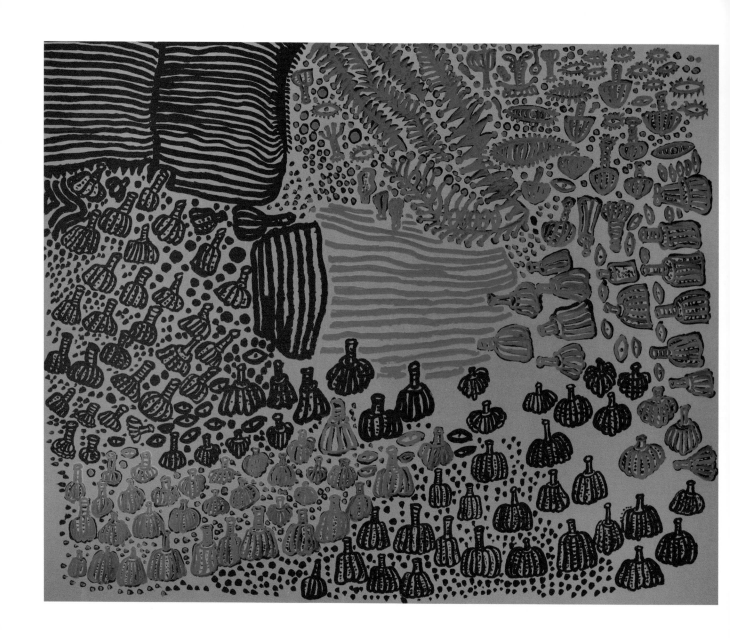

南瓜之夢

壓克力、畫布
130.3x162cm
2012

PUMPKIN'S DREAM

acrylic on canvas
130.3x162cm
2012

清晨，太陽自地平線升起
壓克力、畫布
162x162cm
2009

MORNING, THE SUN HAS RISEN ABOVE
THE HORIZON
acrylic on canvas
162x162cm
2009

向宇宙中的太陽致敬
壓克力、畫布
162x162cm
2010

TRIBUTE TO THE SUN
IN THE COSMOS
acrylic on canvas
162x162cm
2010

水中嬉戲
壓克力、畫布
162x162cm
2010

FROLICKING WITH WATER
acrylic on canvas
162x162cm
2010

女人聚會
壓克力、畫布
162x162cm
2012

A GATHERING OF WOMEN
acrylic on canvas
162x162cm
2012

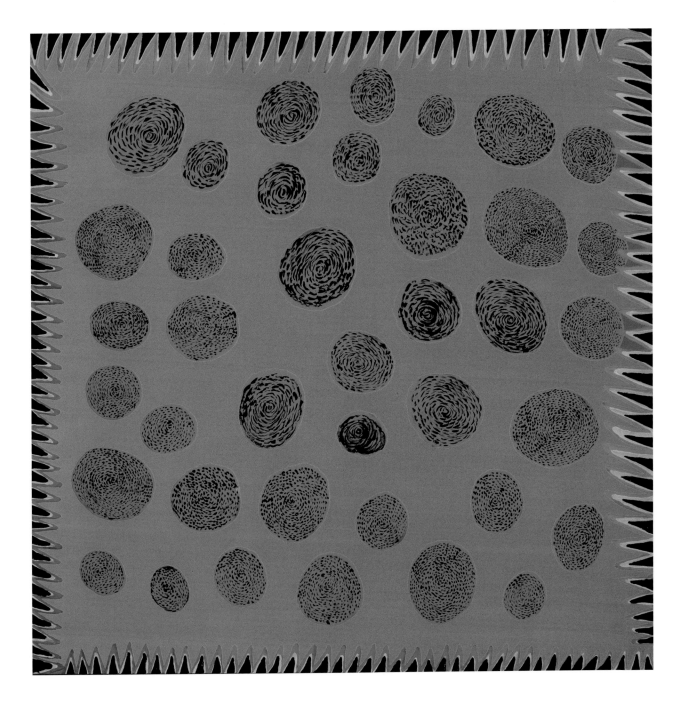

暮光中的星塵
壓克力、畫布
162x162cm
2012

STARDUST IN THE EVENING GLOW
acrylic on canvas
162x162cm
2012

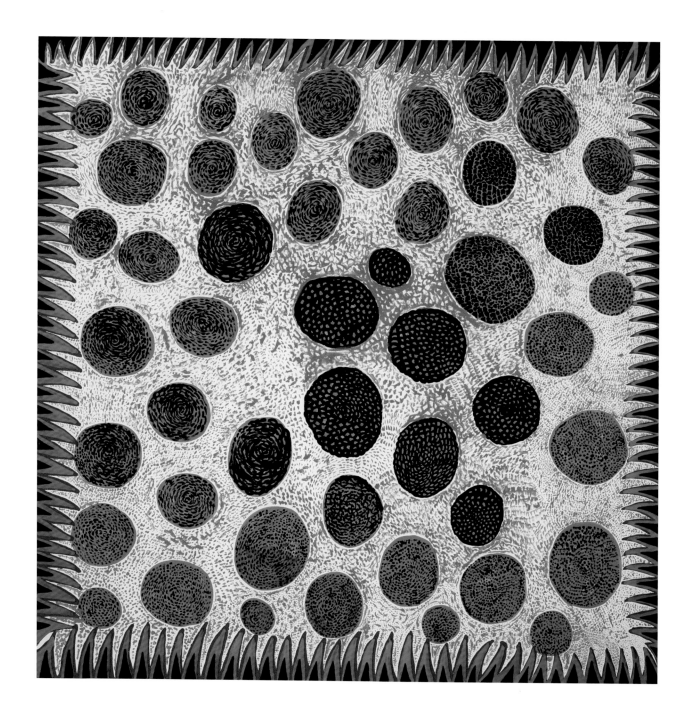

夜晚的星塵
壓克力、畫布
162x162cm
2012

STARDUST AT NIGHT
acrylic on canvas
162x162cm
2012

我放聲哭喊
壓克力、畫布
162x162cm
2012

I AM CRYING OUT
acrylic on canvas
162x162cm
2012

春
壓克力、畫布
162x162cm
2012

SPRING

acrylic on canvas
162x162cm
2012

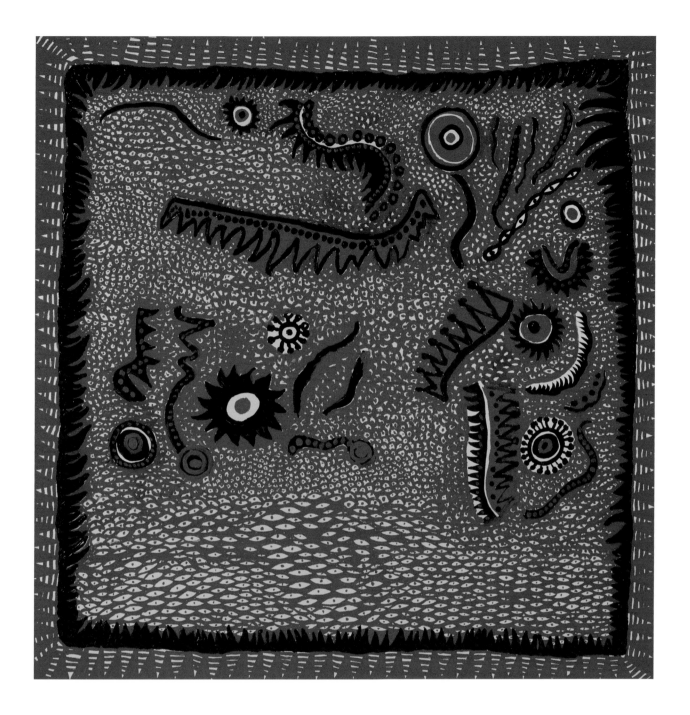

邂逅心中的溫柔
壓克力、畫布
162x162cm
2012

AN ENCOUNTER
WITH THE TENDERNESS OF HEART
acrylic on canvas
162x162cm
2012

奮戰過後，我想在宇宙盡頭死去
壓克力、畫布
162x162cm
2010

AFTER THE BATTLE,
I WANT TO DIE AT THE END OF THE UNIVERSE
acrylic on canvas
162x162cm
2010

睜大雙眼觀賞節慶

壓克力、畫布
194x194cm
2010

WATCHING A FESTIVAL
WITH WIDE-OPEN EYES

acrylic on canvas
194x194cm
2010

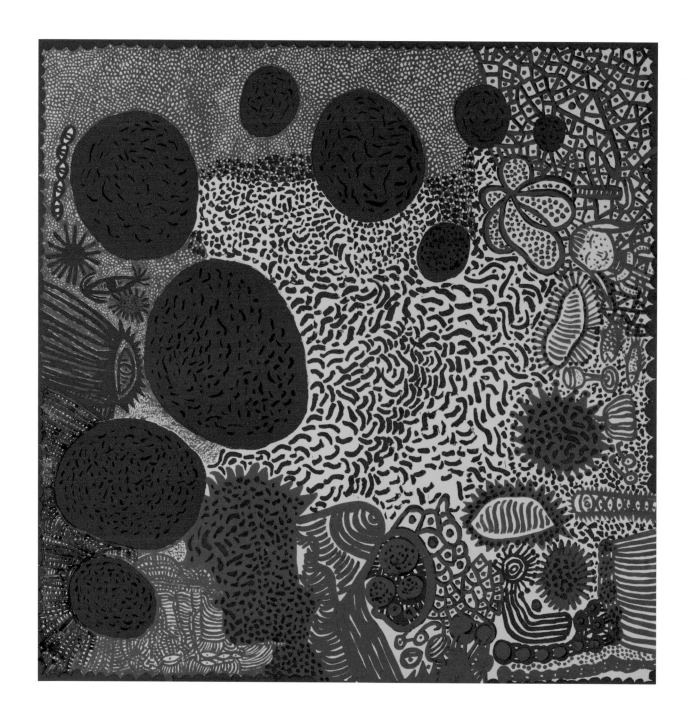

節慶餘波
壓克力、畫布
194x194cm
2010

AFTERMATH OF A FESTIVAL
acrylic on canvas
194x194cm
2010

日照光輝
壓克力、畫布
194x194cm
2013

RADIANCE OF THE SUN
acrylic on canvas
194x194cm
2013

在幸福的天空下
壓克力、畫布
194x194cm
2013

UNDER THE SKY OF HAPPINESS
acrylic on canvas
194x194cm
2013

春天來到女人身邊
壓克力、畫布
194x194cm
2013

SPRING HAS COME TO THE WOMEN
acrylic on canvas
194x194cm
2013

暮光中的花園
壓克力、畫布
194x194cm
2012

FLOWER GARDEN
IN THE EVENING GLOW
acrylic on canvas
194x194cm
2012

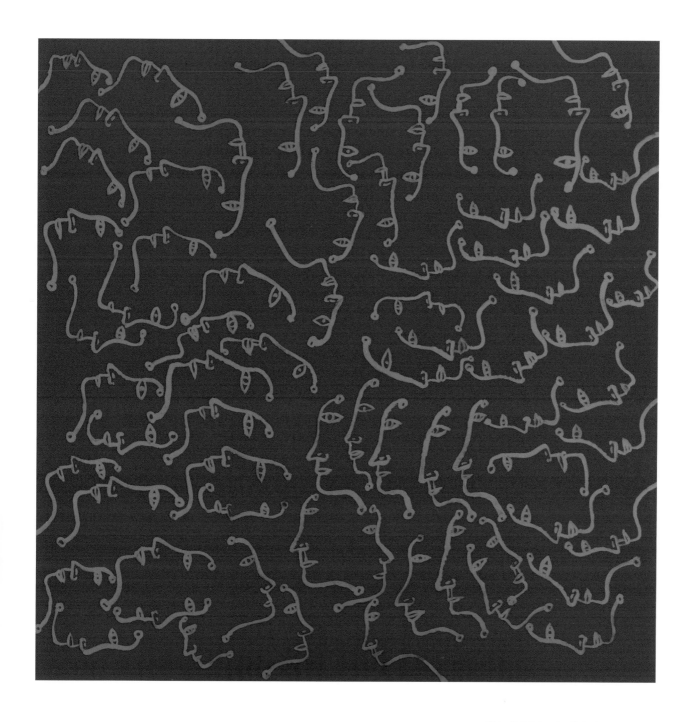

愛如此誘人，但世界卻爭戰不休

壓克力、畫布
194x194cm
2010

LOVE IS SO GLAMOROUS,
BUT THE WORLD IS ENGAGED IN WARS ALL THE TIME

acrylic on canvas
194x194cm
2010

我愛-眼睛
壓克力、畫布
194x194cm
2013

I LOVE-EYES
acrylic on canvas
194x194cm
2013

愛的開端

壓克力、畫布
194x194cm
2010

BEGINNING OF LOVE

acrylic on canvas
194x194cm
2010

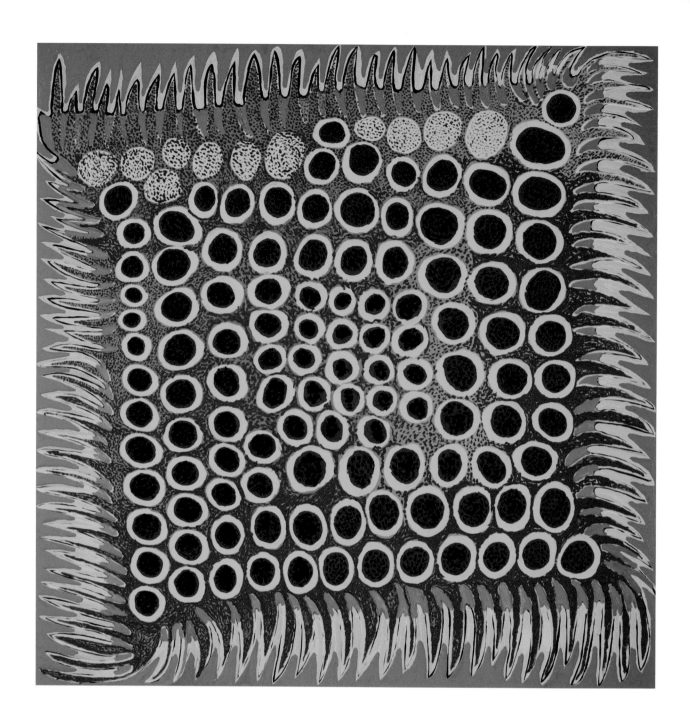

上帝的殿堂
壓克力、畫布
194x194cm
2012

THE PLACE FOR GOD
acrylic on canvas
194x194cm
2012

星辰棲居之所

壓克力、畫布
194x194cm
2012

DWELLING OF STARS

acrylic on canvas
194x194cm
2012

豔陽高照之日
壓克力、畫布
194x194cm
2013

THE DAY THE SUN WAS SHINING
acrylic on canvas
194x194cm
2013

活在人世間
壓克力、畫布
194x194cm
2013

LIVING IN THE WORLD OF PEOPLE
acrylic on canvas
194x194cm
2013

永恆的愛
LOVE FOREVER

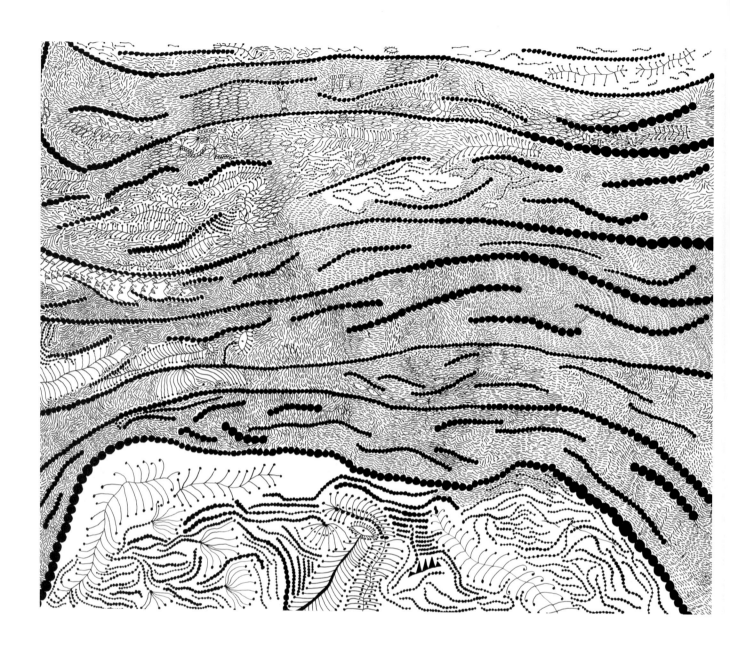

春之甦醒
絹印、畫布
130.3x162cm
2005

AWAKENING OF SPRING [TWSHON]

silkscreen on canvas
130.3x162cm
2005

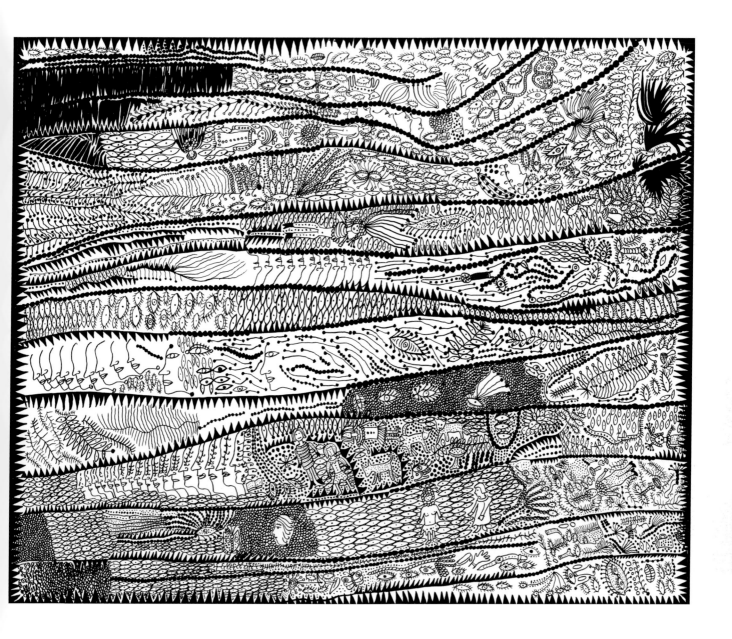

美好的夜
絹印、畫布
130.3x162cm
2005

LOVELY NIGHT [ABCTW]
silkscreen on canvas
130.3x162cm
2005

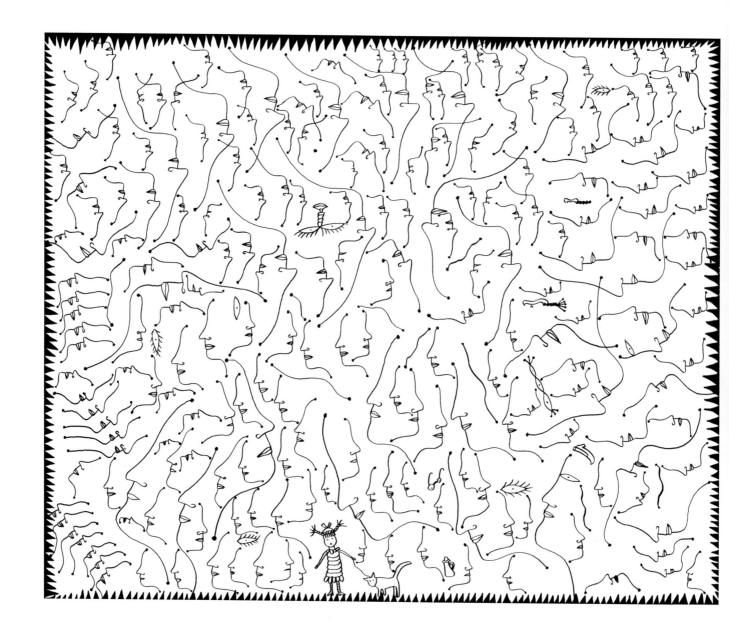

戀人
絹印、畫布
130.3x162cm
2005

LOVERS
silkscreen on canvas
130.3x162cm
2005

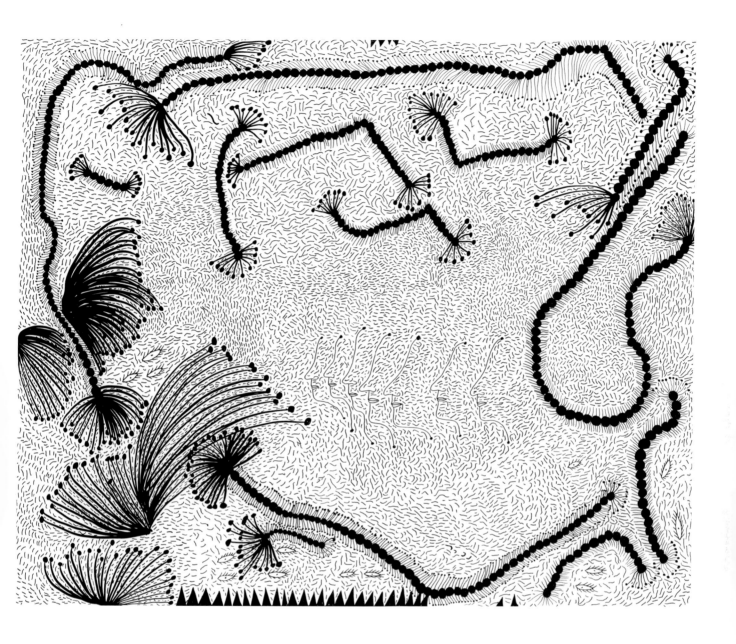

花瓣
絹印、畫布
130.3x162cm
2005

FLOWER PETALS [AWSHTS]
silkscreen on canvas
130.3x162cm
2005

午夜之眠
絹印、畫布
130.3x162cm
2005

MIDNIGHT SLEEP [OPESSA]
silkscreen on canvas
130.3x162cm
2005

派對過後
絹印、畫布
130.3x162cm
2005

AFTER THE PARTY [SOXTE]
silkscreen on canvas
130.3x162cm
2005

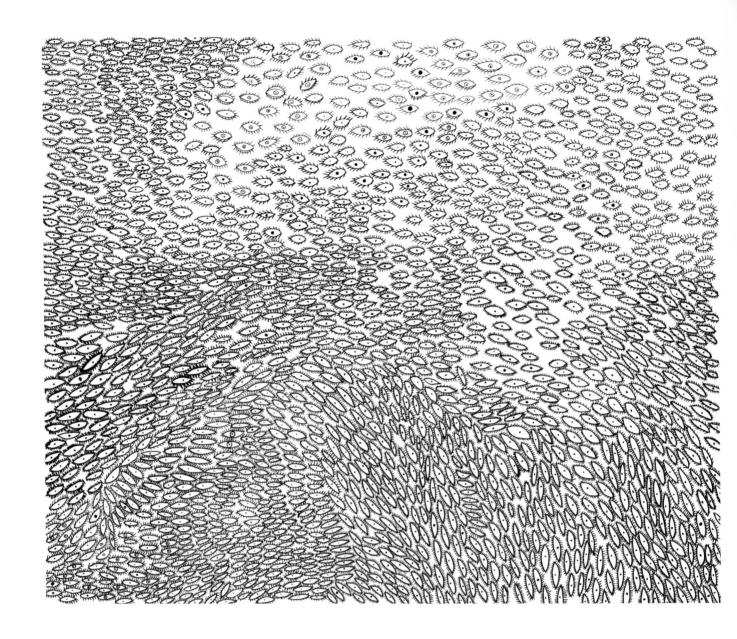

一千雙眼

絹印、畫布

130.3x162cm

2005

ONE-THOUSAND-EYES [TWOXZ]

silkscreen on canvas

130.3x162cm

2005

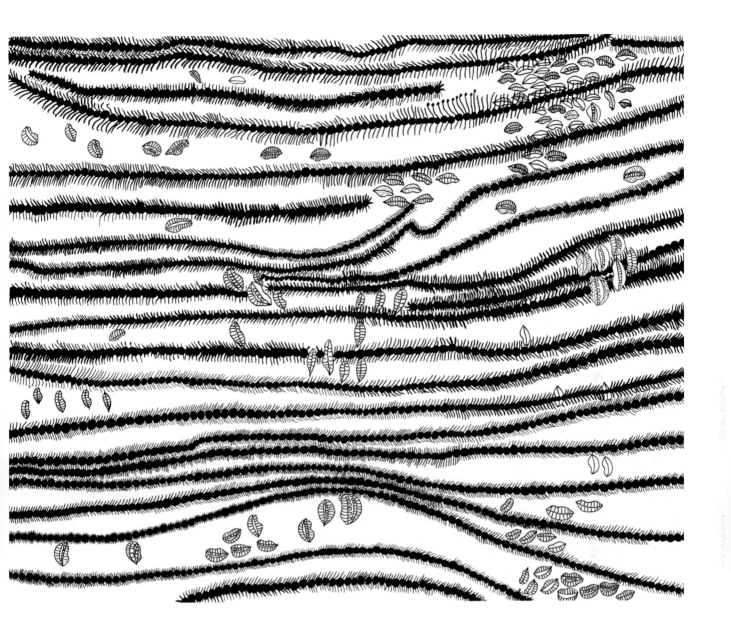

漂浮浪中之唇
絹印、畫布
130.3x162cm
2005

LIPS FLOATING IN THE WAVES [TOWHC]
silkscreen on canvas
130.3x162cm
2005

晨浪
絹印、畫布
130.3x162cm
2005

MORNING WAVES [TEXHT]
silkscreen on canvas
130.3x162cm
2005

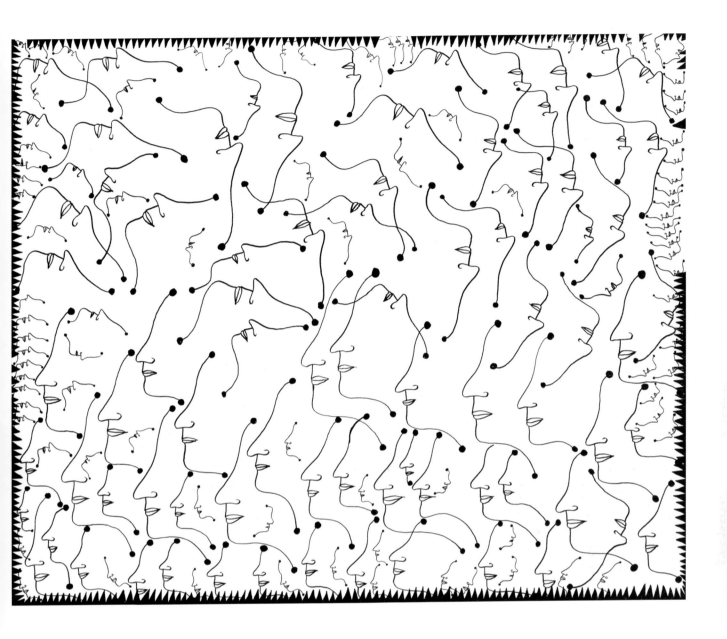

夢中的女人
絹印、畫布
130.3x162cm
2005

WOMEN IN A DREAM [TWZSA]
silkscreen on canvas
130.3x162cm
2005

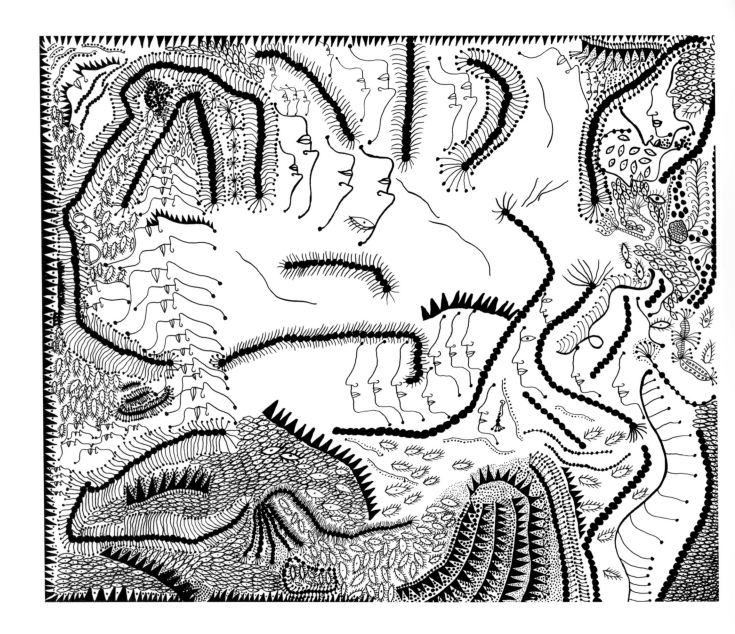

初戀
絹印、畫布
130.3x162cm
2005

FIRST LOVE [SWTUE]
silkscreen on canvas
130.3x162cm
2005

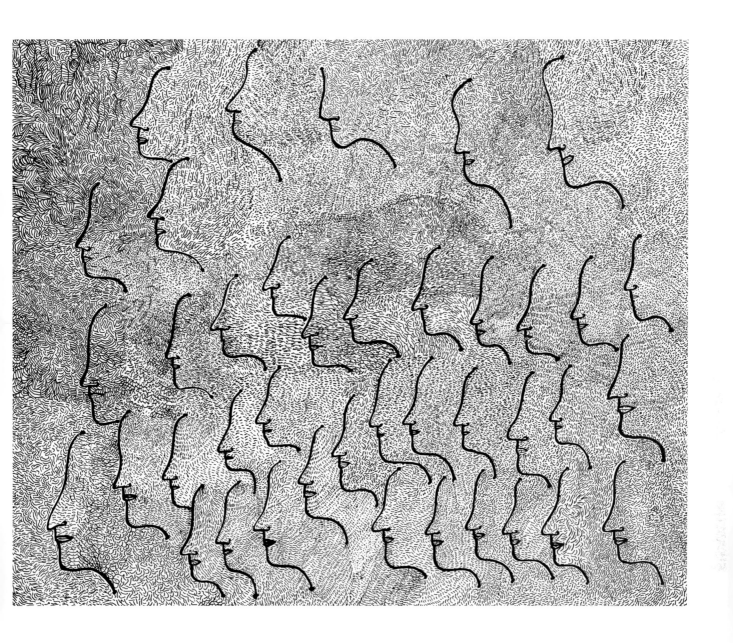

女人殘像
絹印、畫布
130.3x162cm
2005

WOMAN'S AFTERIMAGE [FAOWE]
silkscreen on canvas
130.3x162cm
2005

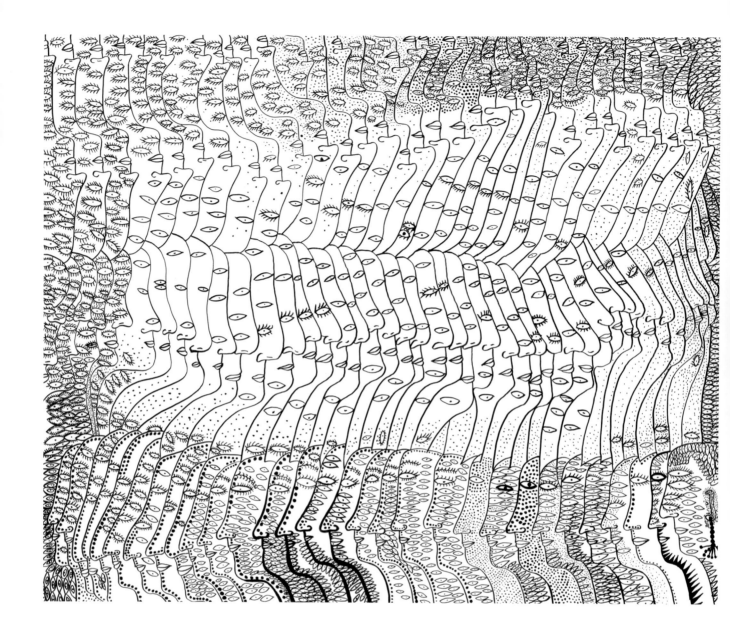

女人
絹印、畫布
130.3x162cm
2005

WOMEN [TTWOP]
silkscreen on canvas
130.3x162cm
2005

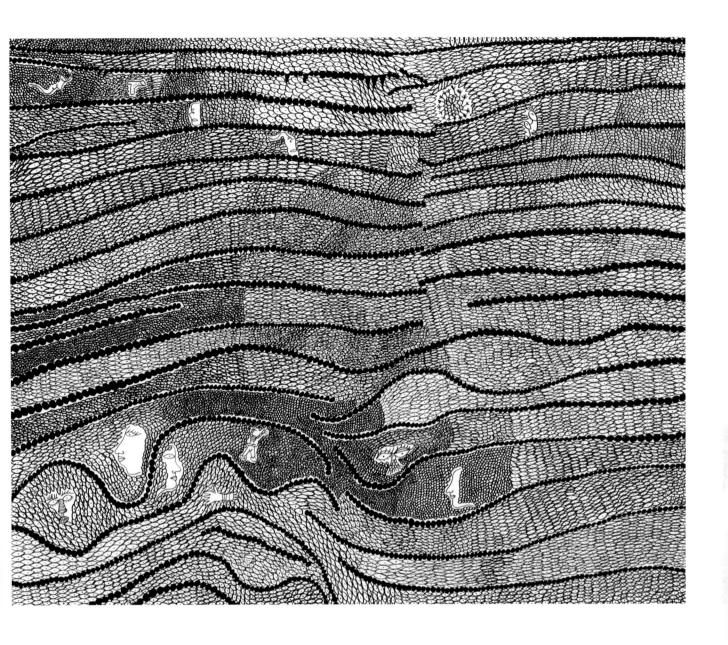

夜的漣漪
絹印、畫布
130.3x162cm
2005

NIGHT RIPPLES [TOWSS]
silkscreen on canvas
130.3x162cm
2005

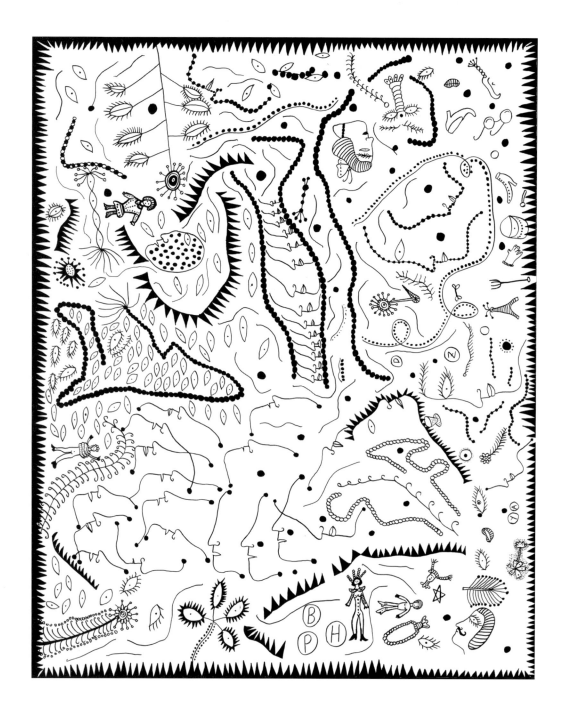

夏日午後
絹印、畫布
162x130.3cm
2005

SUMMER AFTERNOON [FTOPK]

silkscreen on canvas
162x130.3cm
2005

擁擠之群
絹印、畫布
162x130.3cm
2005

THE CROWD [TWXOZ]
silkscreen on canvas
162x130.3cm
2005

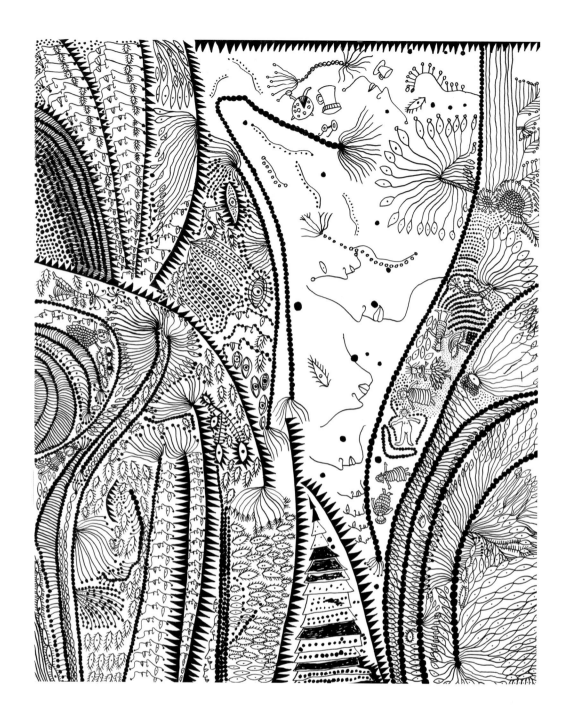

永恆的愛
絹印、畫布
162x130.3cm
2005

LOVE FOREVER [OPXTWE]
silkscreen on canvas
162x130.3cm
2005

女人的世界
絹印、畫布
162x130.3cm
2005

WOMAN'S WORLD [OEWST]
silkscreen on canvas
162x130.3cm
2005

川流之河
絹印、畫布
162x130.3cm
2006

A FLOWING RIVER
silkscreen on canvas
162x130.3cm
2006

女人聚會
絹印、畫布
162x130.3cm
2006

A GATHERING OF WOMEN
silkscreen on canvas
162x130.3cm
2006

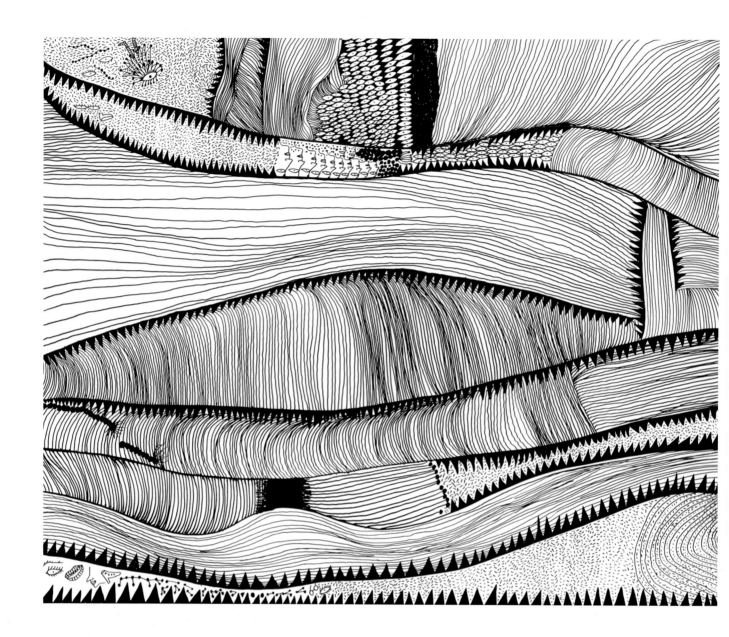

拂曉之浪
絹印、畫布
130.3x162cm
2006

WAVES AT DAYBREAK
silkscreen on canvas
130.3x162cm
2006

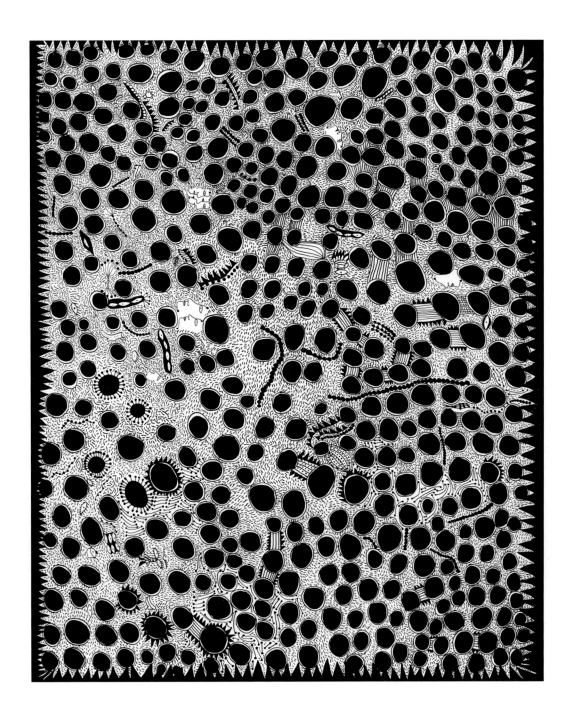

我昨日之夢
絹印、畫布
162x130.3cm
2006

A DREAM I DREAMED YESTERDAY
silkscreen on canvas
162x130.3cm
2006

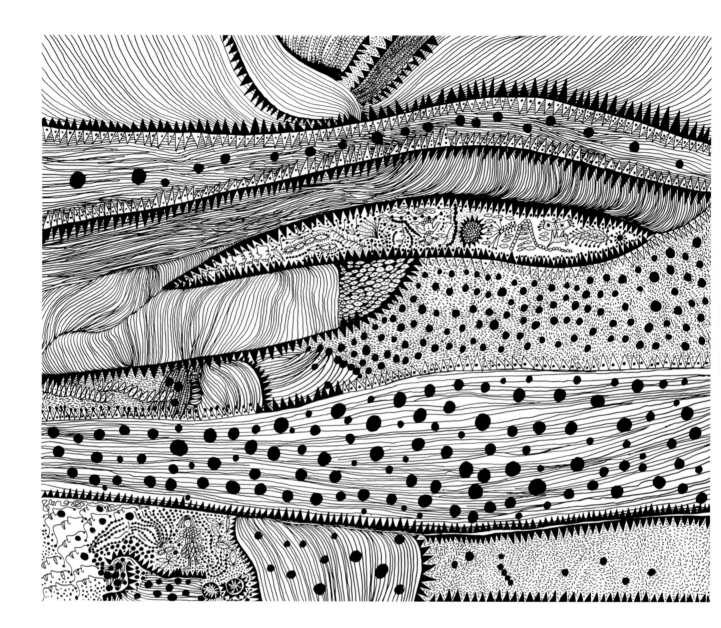

愛的終結
絹印、畫布
130.3x162cm
2006

END OF LOVE
silkscreen on canvas
130.3x162cm
2006

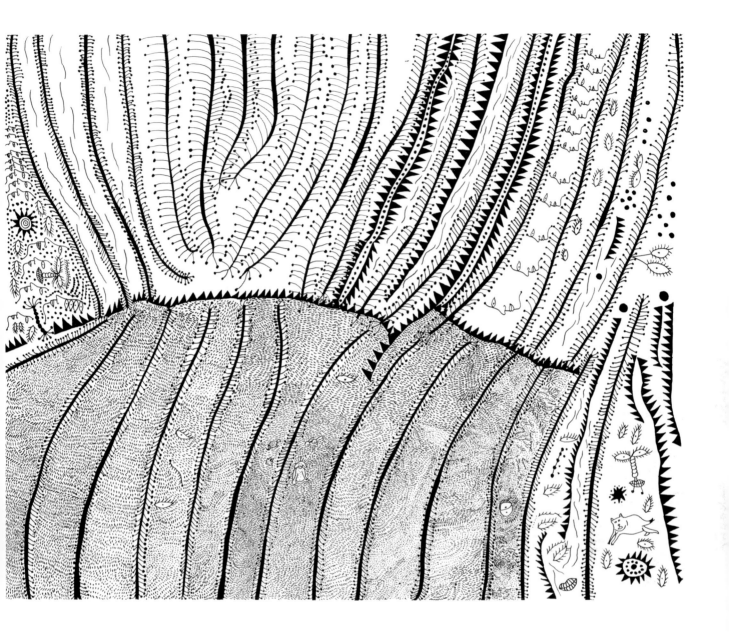

初夏
絹印、畫布
130.3x162cm
2006

EARLY SUMMER [TWPOX]
silkscreen on canvas
130.3x162cm
2006

生命頌歌
絹印、畫布
130.3x162cm
2005

HYMN OF LIFE [BOZA]
silkscreen on canvas
130.3x162cm
2005

永恆的愛
絹印、畫布
130.3x162cm
2004

LOVE FOREVER (TAOW)
silkscreen on canvas
130.3x162cm
2004

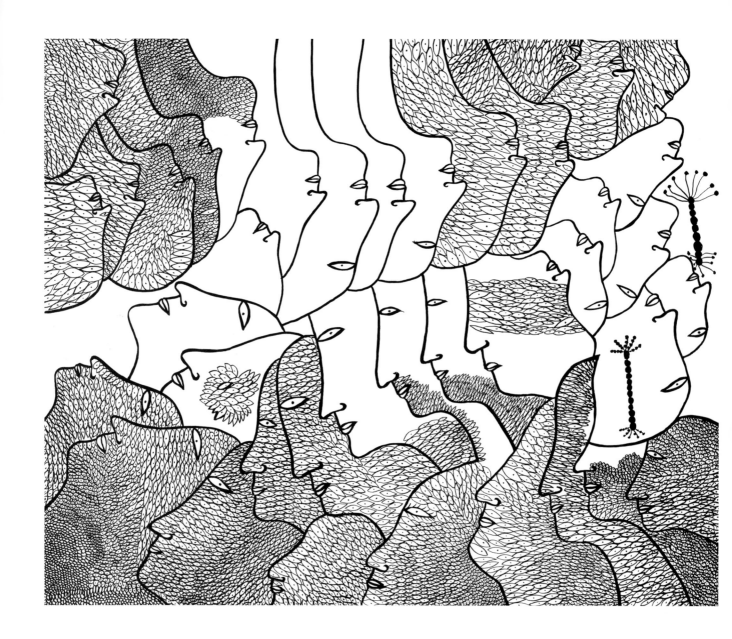

晨已到來
絹印、畫布
130.3x162cm
2005

MORNING IS HERE [TWST]
silkscreen on canvas
130.3x162cm
2005

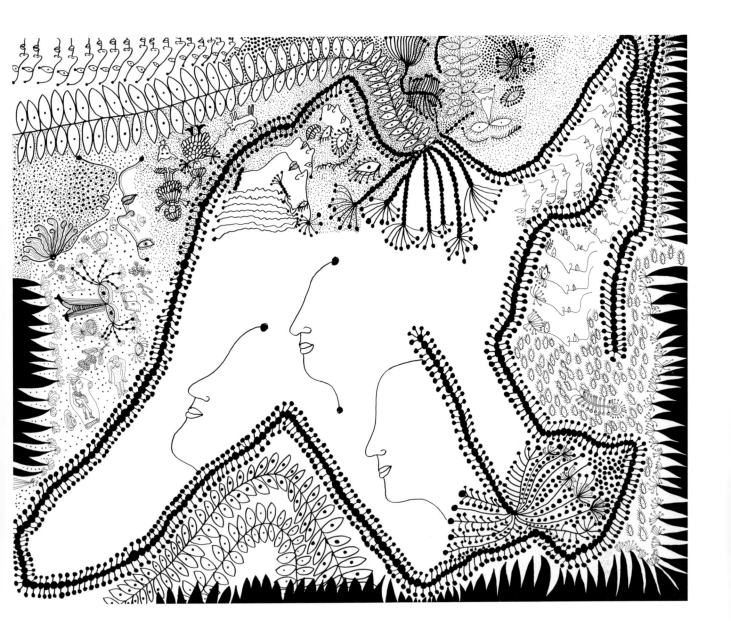

春的到來
絹印、畫布
130.3x162cm
2005

ARRIVAL OF SPRING [QA.B.Z]
silkscreen on canvas
130.3x162cm
2005

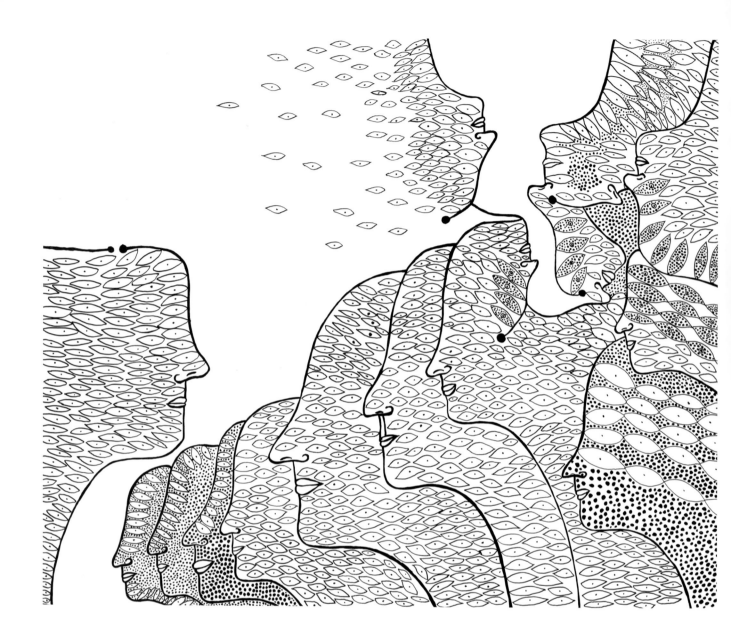

等待春天的女人
絹印、畫布
130.3x162cm
2005

WOMEN WAITING FOR SPRING [TZW]
silkscreen on canvas
130.3x162cm
2005

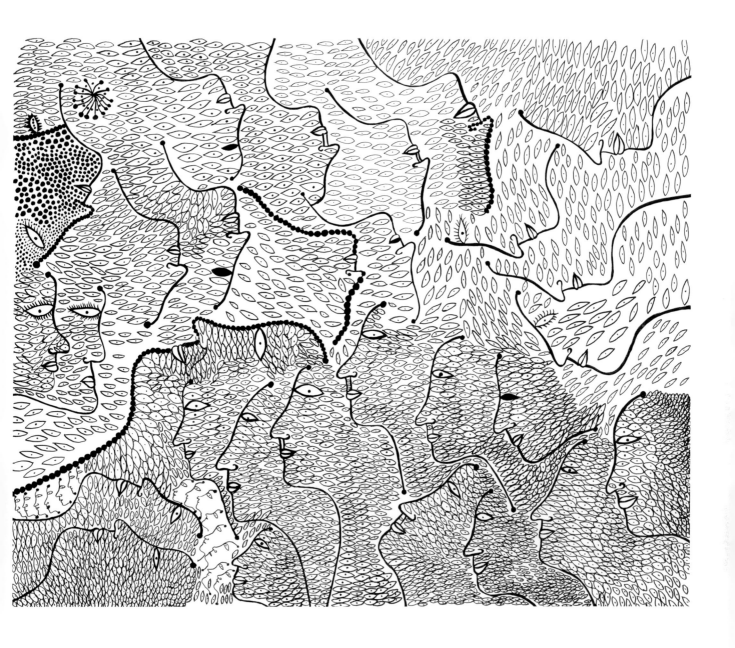

午夜的女人
絹印、畫布
130.3x162cm
2005

WOMEN IN THE MIDNIGHT
silkscreen on canvas
130.3x162cm
2005

花的禮讚
絹印、畫布
162x130.3cm
2006

FLORAL TRIBUTE (TULIPS)
silkscreen on canvas
162x130.3cm
2006

走入原野
絹印、畫布
162x130.3cm
2006

GOING OUT INTO THE FIELD
silkscreen on canvas
162x130.3cm
2006

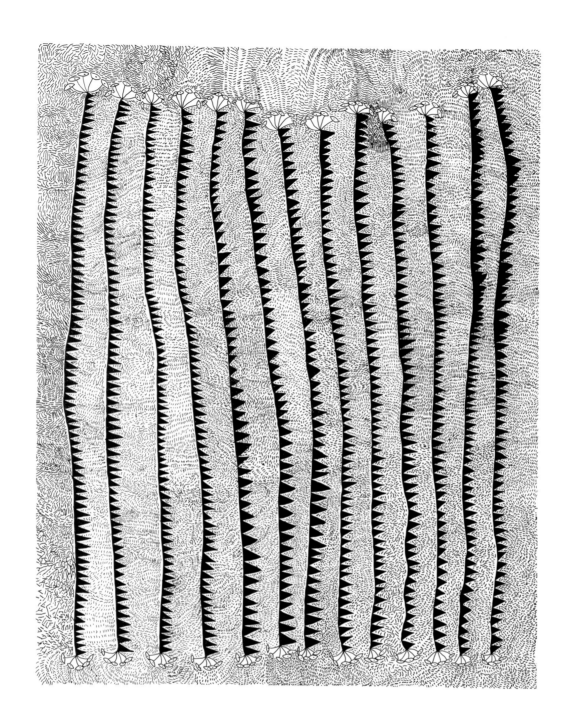

我心中之旗
絹印、畫布
162x130.3cm
2006

FLAG IN MY HEART [TXOZT]

silkscreen on canvas
162x130.3cm
2006

花開紐約

絹印、畫布

162x130.3cm

2005

FLOWERING NEW YORK [OPRT]

silkscreen on canvas

162x130.3cm

2005

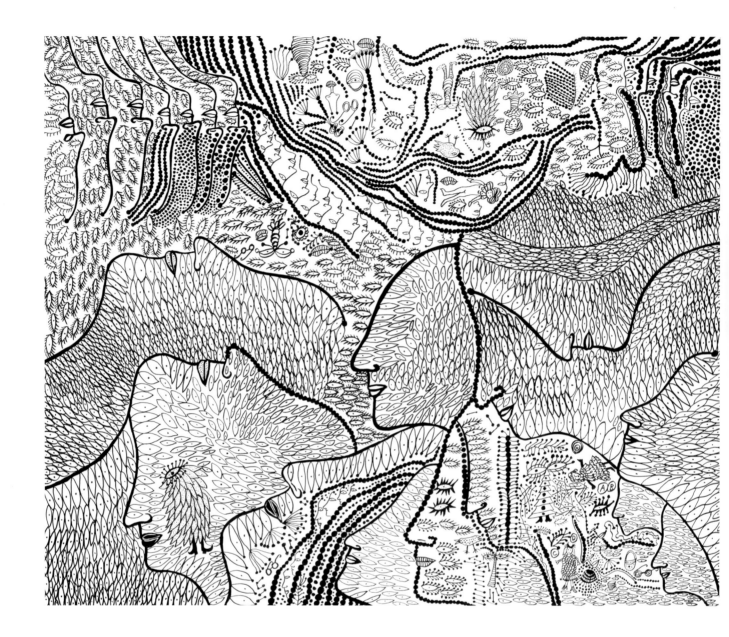

初春之兆

絹印、畫布
130.3x162cm
2005

SIGNS OF EARLY SPRING [T.A.A.Z]

silkscreen on canvas
130.3x162cm
2005

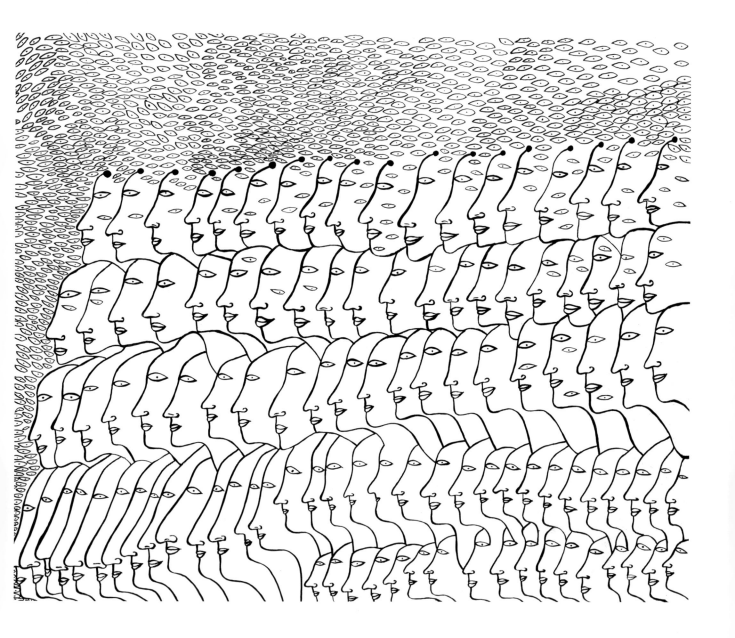

女人的一生
絹印、畫布
130.3x162cm
2005

WOMAN'S LIFE [T.WXO]
silkscreen on canvas
130.3x162cm
2005

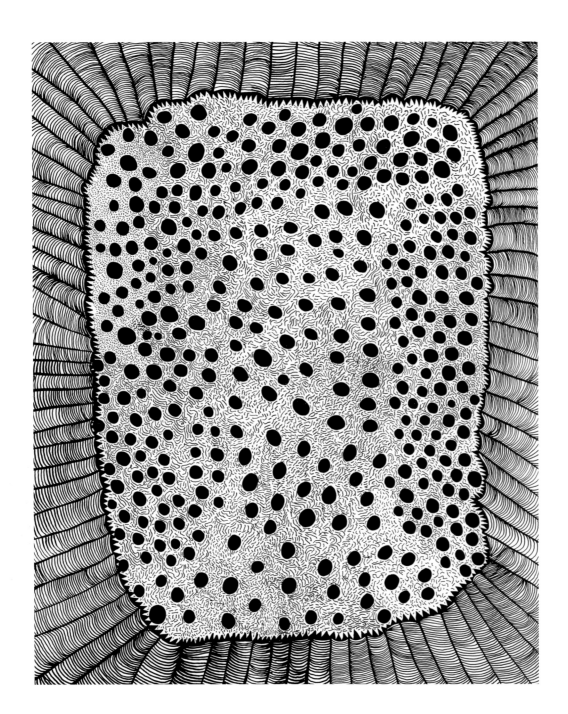

星辰棲居之所
絹印、畫布
162x130.3cm
2007

DWELLING OF STARS [TWXSS]
silkscreen on canvas
162x130.3cm
2007

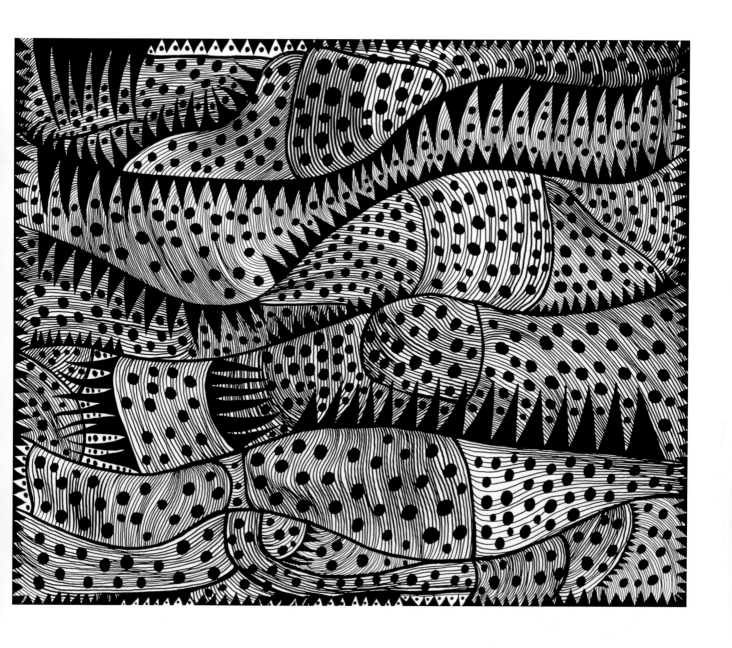

生、老、病、死
絹印、畫布
130.3x162cm
2007

BIRTH, AGING, SICKNESS AND DEATH
[QXPAT]

silkscreen on canvas
130.3x162cm
2007

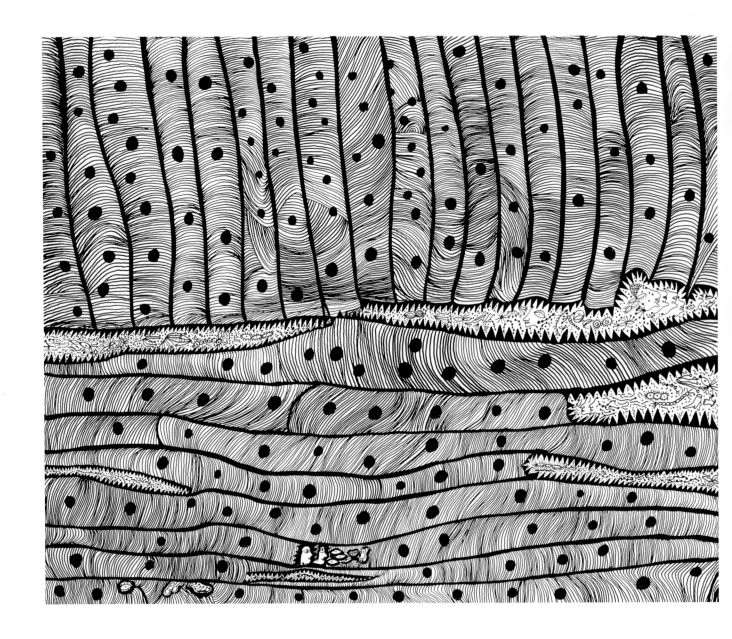

春之兆
絹印、畫布
130.3x162cm
2007

SIGNS OF SPRING [WQZY]
silkscreen on canvas
130.3x162cm
2007

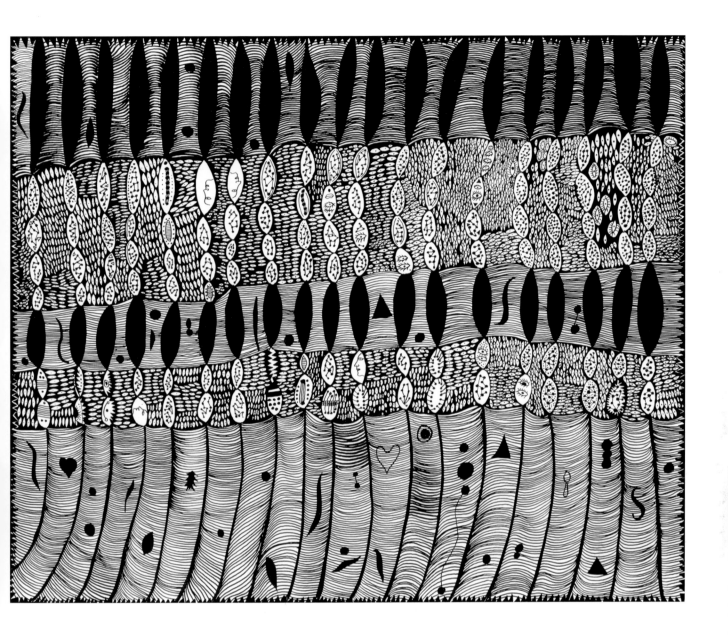

青春標竿
絹印、畫布
130.3x162cm
2007

GUIDEPOST TO YOUTH [HOTWOX]
silkscreen on canvas
130.3x162cm
2007

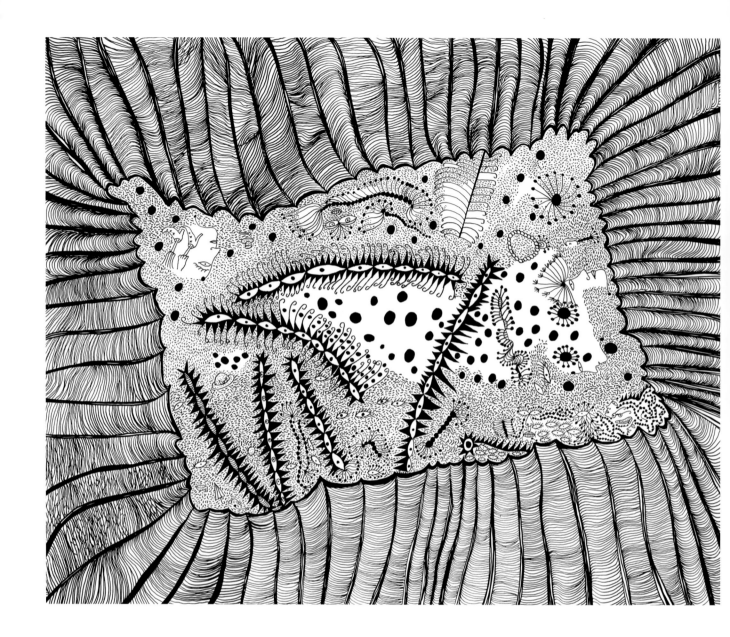

萌芽
絹印、畫布
130.3x162cm
2006

SPROUTING [TOXZS]
silkscreen on canvas
130.3x162cm
2006

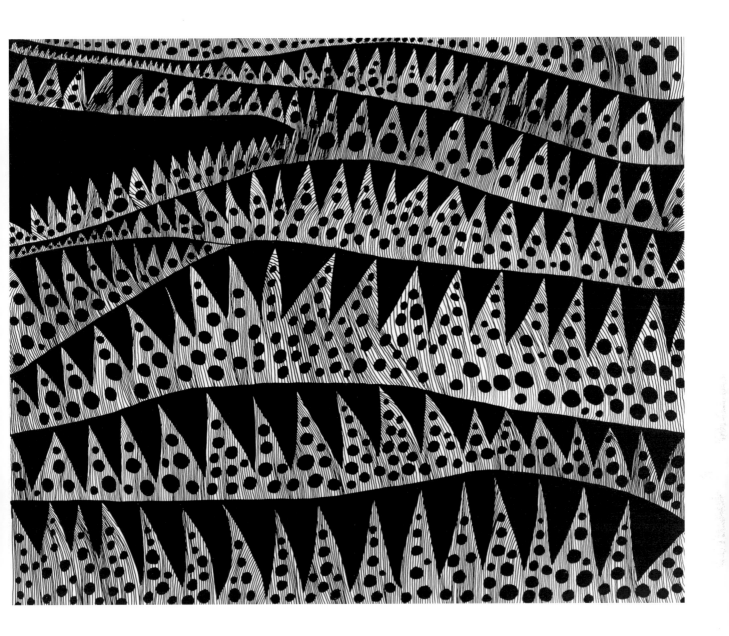

波浪
絹印、畫布
130.3x162cm
2007

WAVES [TWXZO]
silkscreen on canvas
130.3x162cm
2007

宇宙之旅
絹印、畫布
130.3x162cm
2007

JOURNEY TO THE UNIVERSE [TZQMN]
silkscreen on canvas
130.3x162cm
2007

青春時光
絹印、畫布
130.3x162cm
2007

DAYS OF YOUTH [YOZMTO]
silkscreen on canvas
130.3x162cm
2007

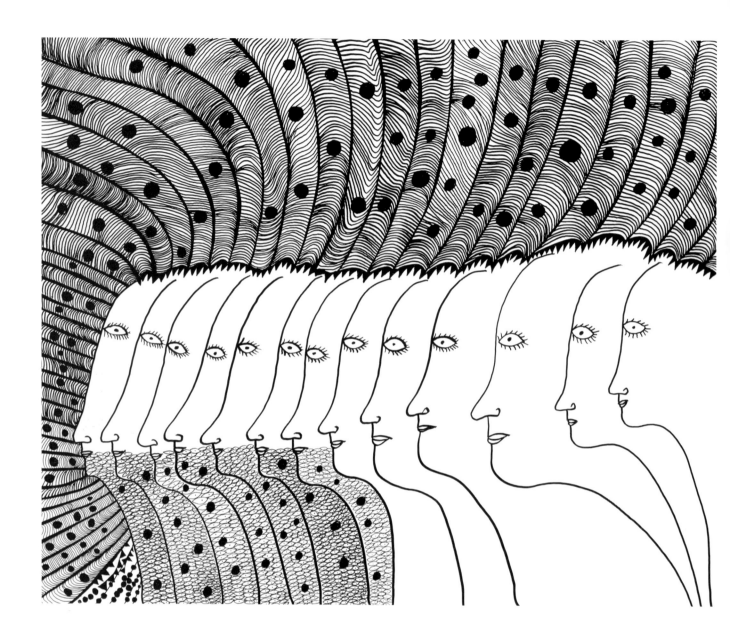

晨之華
絹印、畫布
130.3x162cm
2007

MORNING SPLENDOR [TWHIOW]

silkscreen on canvas
130.3x162cm
2007

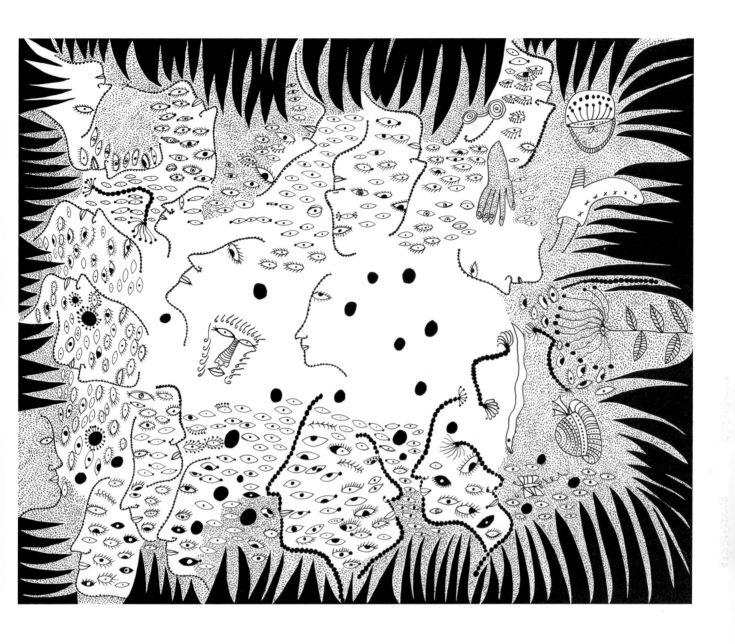

女人的紐約
絹印、畫布
130.3x162cm
2007

WOMEN'S NEW YORK [SSAAWA]

silkscreen on canvas
130.3x162cm
2007

早晨醒來
絹印、畫布
130.3x162cm
2007

WAKING UP IN THE MORNING [TQSTW]
silkscreen on canvas
130.3x162cm
2007

我喜歡自己
絹印、畫布
130.3x162cm
2006

I LIKE MYSELF [TOWHSQ]
silkscreen on canvas
130.3x162cm
2006

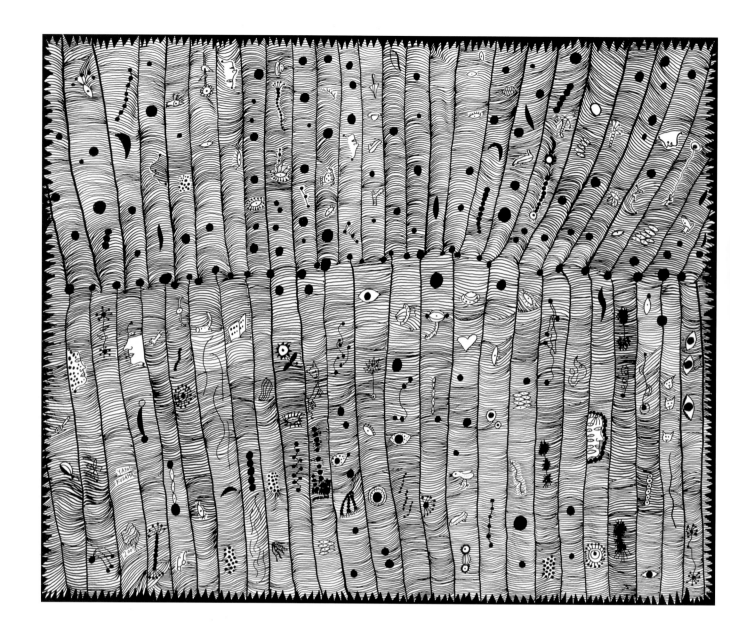

天國入口
絹印、畫布
130.3x162cm
2007

ENTRANCE TO HEAVEN [TQWFV]
silkscreen on canvas
130.3x162cm
2007

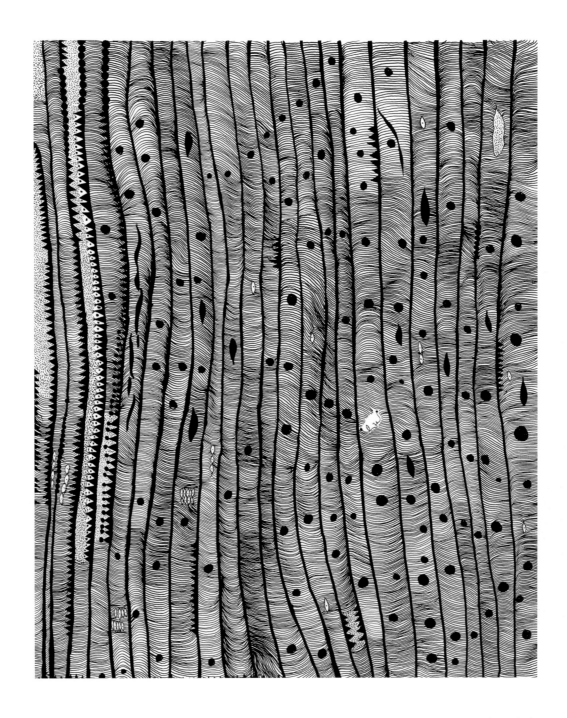

無限宇宙
絹印、畫布
162x130.3cm
2007

INFINITY-COSMOS [TOWEY]
silkscreen on canvas
162x130.3cm
2007

無限的網與點
INFINITY NETS & DOTS

藍色的網
壓克力、畫布
162x130.3cm
2012

BLUE NETS [WOSNE]
acrylic on canvas
162x130.3cm
2012

無限的網
壓克力、畫布
130.3x130.3cm
2011

INFINITY NETS [ASWQH]
acrylic on canvas
130.3x130.3cm
2011

無限的網
壓克力、畫布
194x194cm
2013

INFINITY-NETS [LPDWQ]
acrylic on canvas
194x194cm
2013

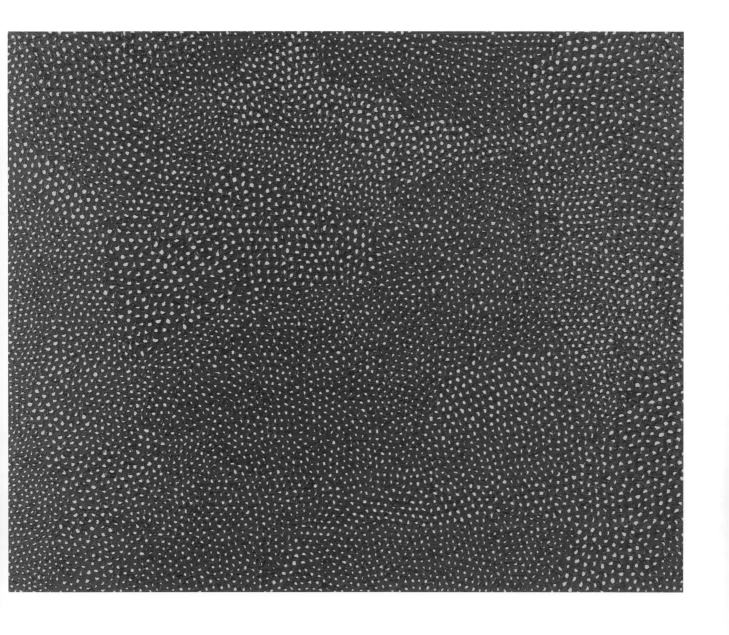

無限的網
壓克力、畫布
130.3x162cm
2011

INFINITY NETS [PADWH]
acrylic on canvas
130.3x162cm
2011

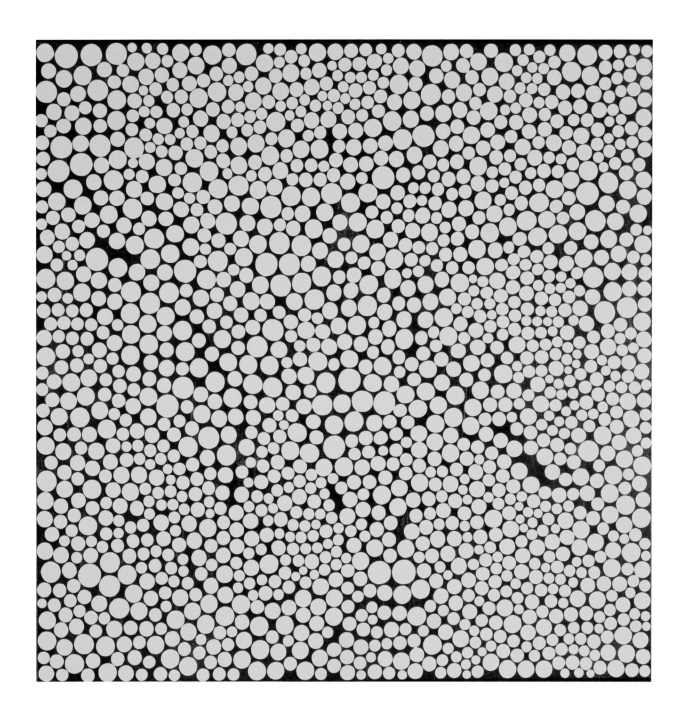

圓點執念
壓克力、畫布
194x194cm
2013

DOTS OBSESSION [FOPMU]
acrylic on canvas
194x194cm
2013

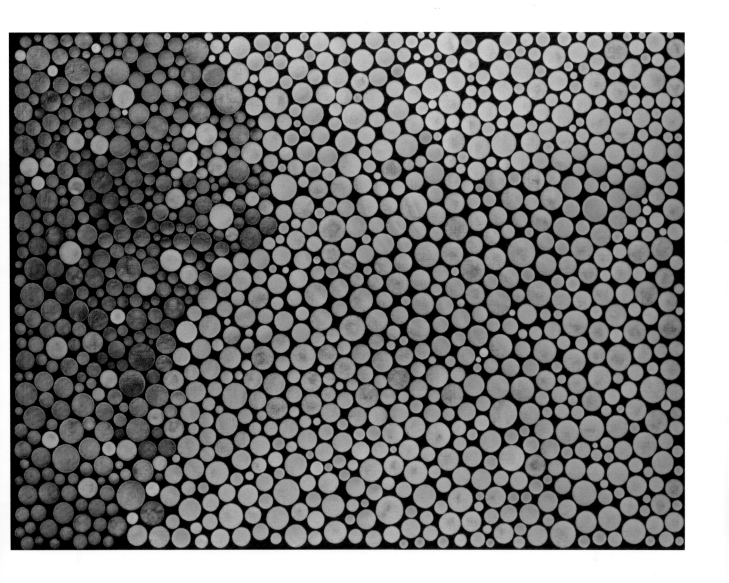

圓點

壓克力、畫布
97x130.3cm
2008

DOTS [ABCDEF]

acrylic on canvas
97x130.3cm
2008

無限雙點
壓克力、畫布
145.5x112cm
2013

INFINITY DOUBLE DOTS
acrylic on canvas
145.5x112cm
2013

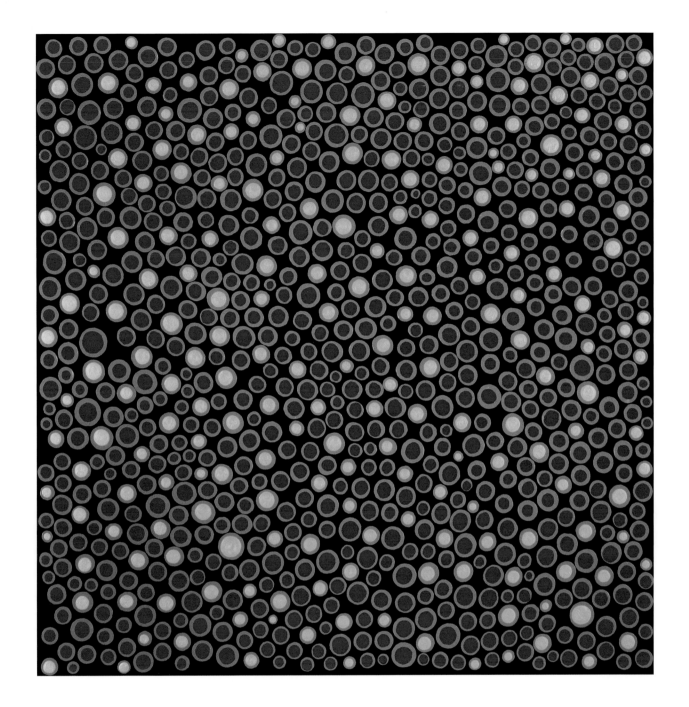

無限的網
壓克力、畫布
145.5x145.5cm
2012

INFINITY DOTS [AHPRUS]
acrylic on canvas
145.5x145.5cm
2012

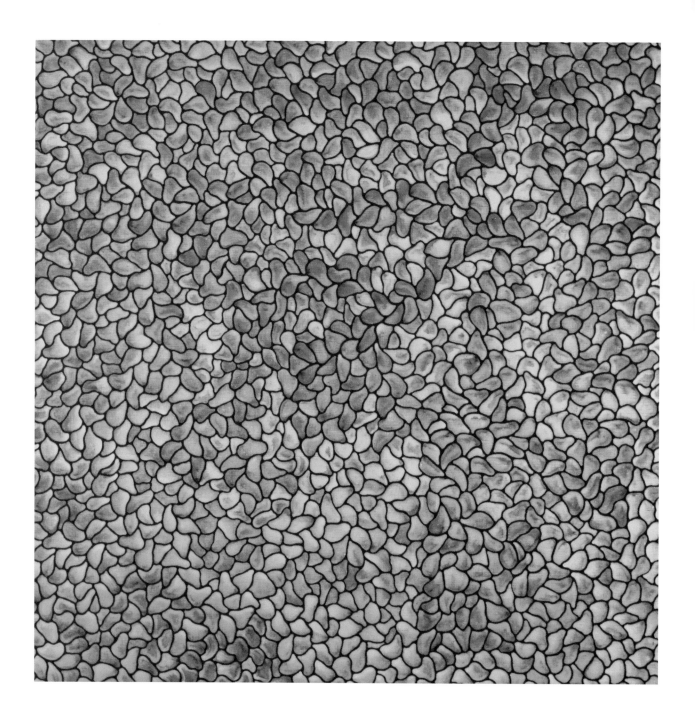

雲
壓克力、畫布
130.3x130.3cm
2008

THE CLOUDS [PSSOW]
acrylic on canvas
130.3x130.3cm
2008

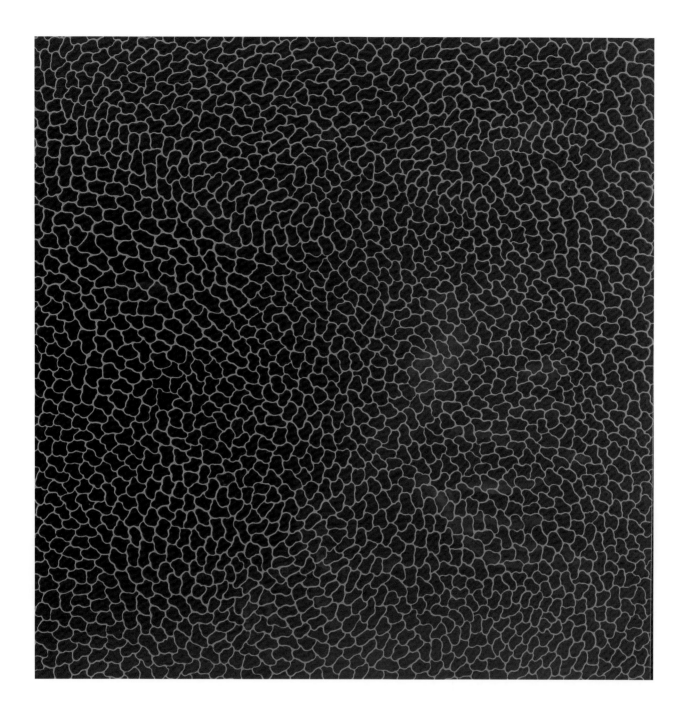

無限的網
壓克力、畫布
145.5x145.5cm
2012

INFINITY NETS [QTAB]
acrylic on canvas
145.5x145.5cm
2012

星之消融
壓克力、畫布
259x194cm
2010

OBLITERATION OF STARS (COPPER)
acrylic on canvas
259x194cm
2010

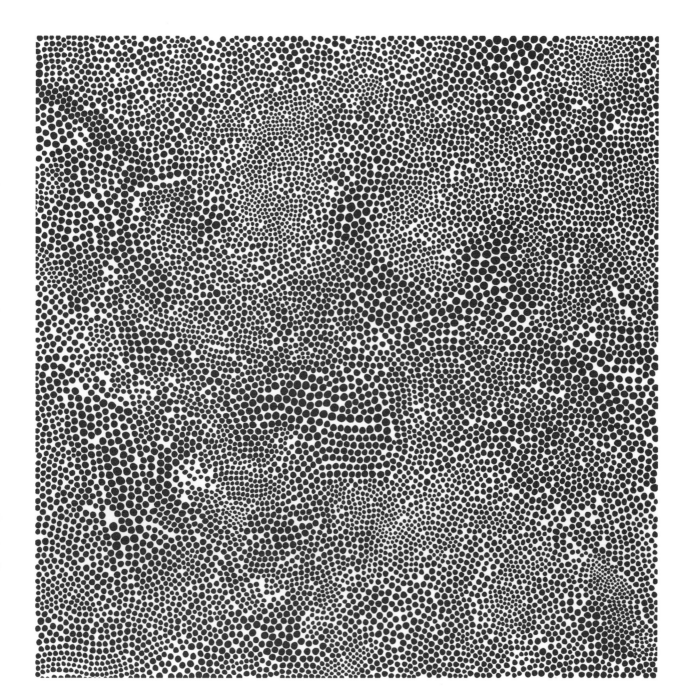

紅點
壓克力、畫布
194x194cm
2013

RED DOTS [TVRS]
acrylic on canvas
194x194cm
2013

無限的網
壓克力、畫布
162x162cm
2013

INFINITY-NETS[ZAALO]
acrylic on canvas
162x162cm
2013

無限的網
壓克力、畫布
227.3x181.8cm
2013

IINFINITY NETS [AWPFE]
acrylic on canvas
227.3x181.8cm
2013

無限的網
壓克力、畫布
227.3x181.8cm
2013

INFINITY NETS [SHOMC]
acrylic on canvas
227.3x181.8cm
2013

無限的網
壓克力、畫布
3片：每片194x130.3cm
2006

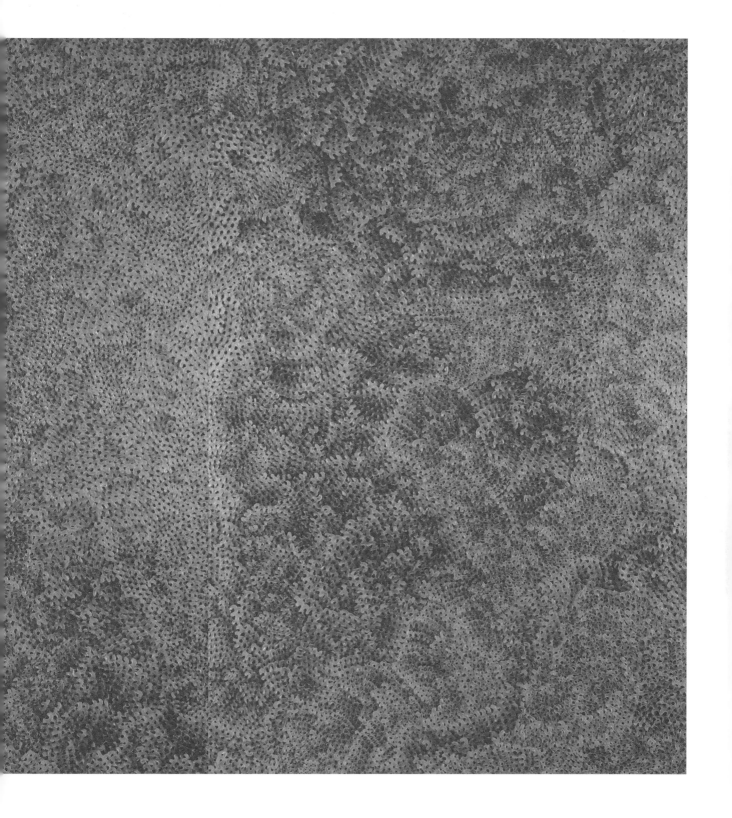

INFINITY NETS [TWHOQ]
acrylic on canvas
3 panels: each 194x130.3cm
2006

無限的網
壓克力、畫布
3片：每片145.5x112cm
2008

INFINITY NETS [OOXSAN]
acrylic on canvas
3 panels:each 145.5x112cm
2008

輪迴
壓克力、畫布
4片：每片194x130.3cm
2011

TRANSMIGRATION
acrylic on canvas
4 panels: each 194x130.3cm
2011

作品檢索
List of works

小健二
KENJI-CHAN
玻璃纖維、聚氨酯塗料
F.R.P.(Fiberglass Reinforced
Plastic), urethane paint
60x134xH94cm
2013

無限鏡屋-靈魂閃耀
Infinity Mirrored Room -
Brilliance of the Souls
鏡面、木板、LED燈、金屬、
壓克力板、水
mirror, wooden panel, LED, metal,
acrylic panel, water
415x415xH 287.4cm
2014

圓點執念
Dots Obsession
複合媒材 mixed media
尺寸可變 dimension variable
2015

小次郎
JIRO-CHAN
玻璃纖維、聚氨酯塗料
F.R.P.(Fiberglass Reinforced
Plastic), urethane paint
48x101xH80cm
2013

無限鏡屋-永恆的愛
Infinity Mirrored Room-
Love Foreve
鏡子、金屬、電燈泡、木
mirror, metal, electric bulb, wood
210x205xH240cm
1994

為摯愛的鬱金香永恆祈禱
With All My Love for the Tulips,
I Pray Forever
金屬、玻璃纖維、聚氨酯塗料、貼紙
metal, F.R.P.(FiberglassReinforced
Plastic), urethane paint, stickers
201x170xH295cm
181x170xH235cm
210x170xH229.5cm
2013

小童
TOKO-CHAN
玻璃纖維、聚氨酯塗料
F.R.P.(Fiberglass Reinforced
Plastic), urethane paint
48x101xH80cm
2013

重複視覺，陽具之舟
Repetitive-Vision, Phallus-Boat
填充縫製合成布料、
發泡橡膠與塑膠、海報
stuffed sewn synthetic fabric,
foam rubber and plastic, posters
boat:330x145xH70cm,
oars:each 200cm
1966/2015

自戀庭園
Narcissus Garden
不鏽鋼球
stainless steel sphere
1,500 spheres (φ30cm)
1966/2015

小歐
OHCHAN
玻璃纖維、聚氨酯塗料
F.R.P.(Fiberglass Reinforced
Plastic), urethane paint
28x88xH68cm
2013

天國之梯
Ladder to Heaven
鏡面、金屬、燈、纖維繩
mirror,metal, lamp, fibercable
dia.150xH360cm
2012

我在這裡，但什麼也不是
I'm Here, but Nothing
乙烯貼紙、紫外線螢光燈、
傢俱、居家用品
vinyl stickers, ultraviolet fluorescent
lights, furniture, household objects
尺寸可變 dimension variable
2015

小正
SHO-CHAN
玻璃纖維、聚氨酯塗料
F.R.P.(Fiberglass Reinforced
Plastic), urethane paint
28x88xH68cm
2013

再生時刻
The Moment of Regeneration
縫製布料、聚氨胺泡棉、
壓克力、木
Sewn fabric, urethane foam,
acrylic, wood
尺寸可變 dimension variable
2004

小龍
TATCHAN
玻璃纖維、聚氨酯塗料
F.R.P.(Fiberglass Reinforced
Plastic), urethane paint
60x134xH94cm
2013

消融之屋
The Obliteration Room
傢俱、白色油漆、圓點貼紙
furniture, white paint, dot stickers
尺寸可變 dimension variable
2002-2015

曼哈頓自殺慣犯之歌
Song of a Manhattan Suicide
Addict
錄像（1分24秒）
video(1min.24 sec.)
尺寸可變 dimension variable
2010

大南瓜 / 南瓜 / 南瓜
Great Gigantic Pumpkin
Pumpkin / Pumpkin
玻璃纖維、聚氨酯塗料、金屬
F.R.P.(FiberglassReinforced
Plastic), urethane paint,
φ260xH250cm
φ200xH205cm
φ130xH125cm
2014 / 2013 / 2013

我的永恆靈魂
MY ETERNAL SOUL

南瓜之夢
PUMPKIN'S DREAM
壓克力、畫布
acrylic on canvas
130.3x162cm
2012

我放聲哭喊
I AM CRYING OUT
壓克力、畫布
acrylic on canvas
162x162cm
2012

想要將我所有的愛，
以及夜晚的夢都吃下去
ALL ABOUT MY LOVE, AND I LONG
TO EAT A DREAM OF THE NIGHT
壓克力、畫布
acrylic on canvas
130.3x162cm
2009

清晨，太陽自地平線升起
MORNING, THE SUN HAS RISEN
ABOVE THE HORIZON
壓克力、畫布
acrylic on canvas
162x162cm
2009

春
SPRING
壓克力、畫布
acrylic on canvas
162x162cm
2012

花季邂逅
AN ENCOUNTER WITH A FLOW-
ERING SEASON
壓克力、畫布
acrylic on canvas
130.3x162cm
2009

向宇宙中的太陽致敬
TRIBUTE TO THE SUN IN THE
COSMOS
壓克力、畫布
acrylic on canvas
162x162cm
2010

邂逅心中的溫柔
AN ENCOUNTER
WITH THE TENDERNESS OF
HEART
壓克力、畫布
acrylic on canvas
162x162cm
2012

遠在宇宙之外追求真理的閃亮
之星黯淡無光，我越探尋真
理，它們越璀璨
SHINING STARS IN PURSUIT OF THE TRUTH
ARE OFF IN THE DISTANCE BEYOND
UNIVERSE, THE MORE I SOUGHT THE TRUTH,
BRIGHTER THEY SHONE
壓克力、畫布
acrylic on canvas
130.3x162cm
2009

水中嬉戲
FROLICKING WITH WATER
壓克力、畫布
acrylic on canvas
162x162cm
2010

奮戰過後，我想在宇宙盡頭
死去
AFTER THE BATTLE, I WANT
TO DIE AT THE END OF THE
UNIVERSE
壓克力、畫布
acrylic on canvas
162x162cm
2010

愛帶著宇宙故事來到地球
LOVE ARRIVES AT THE EARTH
CARRYING WITH IT A TALE OF
THE COSMOS
壓克力、畫布
acrylic on canvas
130.3x162cm
2009

女人聚會
A GATHERING OF WOMEN
壓克力、畫布
acrylic on canvas
162x162cm
2012

睜大雙眼觀賞節慶
WATCHING A FESTIVAL WITH
WIDE-OPEN EYES
壓克力、畫布
acrylic on canvas
194x194cm
2010

綻放
FLOWERING
壓克力、畫布
acrylic on canvas
162x130.3cm
2012

暮光中的星塵
STARDUST IN THE EVENING
GLOW
壓克力、畫布
acrylic on canvas
162x162cm
2012

節慶餘波
AFTERMATH OF A FESTIVAL
壓克力、畫布
acrylic on canvas
194x194cm
2010

在花園中入眠
SLEEPING IN A FLOWER GARDEN
壓克力、畫布
acrylic on canvas
162x130.3cm
2011

夜晚的星塵
STARDUST AT NIGHT
壓克力、畫布
acrylic on canvas
162x162cm
2012

日照光輝
RADIANCE OF THE SUN
壓克力、畫布
acrylic on canvas
194x194cm
2013

在幸福的天空下
UNDER THE SKY OF HAPPINESS
壓克力、畫布
acrylic on canvas
194x194cm
2013

星辰棲居之所
DWELLING OF STARS
壓克力、畫布
acrylic on canvas
194x194cm
2012

花瓣
FLOWER PETALS [AWSHTS]
絹印、畫布
silkscreen on canvas
130.3x162cm
2005

春天來到女人身邊
SPRING HAS COME TO THE
WOMEN
壓克力、畫布
acrylic on canvas
194x194cm
2013

豔陽高照之日
THE DAY THE SUN WAS SHINING
壓克力、畫布
acrylic on canvas
194x194cm
2013

午夜之眠
MIDNIGHT SLEEP [OPESSA]
絹印、畫布
silkscreen on canvas
130.3x162cm
2005

暮光中的花園
FLOWER GARDEN
IN THE EVENING GLOW
壓克力、畫布
acrylic on canvas
194x194cm
2012

活在人世間
LIVING IN THE WORLD OF
PEOPLE
壓克力、畫布
acrylic on canvas
194x194cm
2013

派對過後
AFTER THE PARTY [SOXTE]
絹印、畫布
silkscreen on canvas
130.3x162cm
2005

愛如此誘人，但世界卻爭戰
不休
LOVE IS SO GLAMOROUS, BUT
THE WORLD IS ENGAGED IN
WARS ALL THE TIME
壓克力、畫布
acrylic on canvas
194x194cm
2010

永恆的愛
LOVE FOREVER

一千雙眼
ONE-THOUSAND-EYES [TWOXZ]
絹印、畫布
silkscreen on canvas
130.3x162cm
2005

我愛-眼睛
I LOVE-EYES
壓克力、畫布
acrylic on canvas
194x194cm
2013

春之甦醒
AWAKENING OF SPRING
[TWSHON]
絹印、畫布
silkscreen on canvas
130.3x162cm
2005

漂浮浪中之唇
LIPS FLOATING IN THE WAVES
[TOWHC]
絹印、畫布
silkscreen on canvas
130.3x162cm
2005

愛的開端
BEGINNING OF LOVE
壓克力、畫布
acrylic on canvas
194x194cm
2010

美好的夜
LOVELY NIGHT [ABCTW]
絹印、畫布
silkscreen on canvas
130.3x162cm
2005

晨浪
MORNING WAVES [TEXHT]
絹印、畫布
silkscreen on canvas
130.3x162cm
2005

上帝的殿堂
THE PLACE FOR GOD
壓克力、畫布
acrylic on canvas
194x194cm
2012

戀人
LOVERS
絹印、畫布
silkscreen on canvas
130.3x162cm
2005

夢中的女人
WOMEN IN A DREAM [TWZSA]
絹印、畫布
silkscreen on canvas
130.3x162cm
2005

初戀
FIRST LOVE [SWTUE]
絹印、畫布
silkscreen on canvas
130.3x162cm
2005

女人的世界
WOMAN'S WORLD [OEWST]
絹印、畫布
silkscreen on canvas
162x130.3cm
2005

生命頌歌
HYMN OF LIFE [BOZA]
絹印、畫布
silkscreen on canvas
130.3x162cm
2005

女人殘像
WOMAN'S AFTERIMAGE [FAOWE]
絹印、畫布
silkscreen on canvas
130.3x162cm
2005

川流之河
A FLOWING RIVER
絹印、畫布
silkscreen on canvas
162x130.3cm
2006

永恆的愛
LOVE FOREVER (TAOW)
絹印、畫布
silkscreen on canvas
130.3x162cm
2004

女人
WOMEN [TTWOP]
絹印、畫布
silkscreen on canvas
130.3x162cm
2005

女人聚會
A GATHERING OF WOMEN
絹印、畫布
silkscreen on canvas
162x130.3cm
2006

晨已到來
MORNING IS HERE [TWST]
絹印、畫布
silkscreen on canvas
130.3x162cm
2005

夜的漣漪
NIGHT RIPPLES [TOWSS]
絹印、畫布
silkscreen on canvas
130.3x162cm
2005

拂曉之浪
WAVES AT DAYBREAK
絹印、畫布
silkscreen on canvas
130.3x162cm
2006

春的到來
ARRIVAL OF SPRING [QA.B.Z]
絹印、畫布
silkscreen on canvas
130.3x162cm
2005

夏日午後
SUMMER AFTERNOON [FTOPK]
絹印、畫布
silkscreen on canvas
162x130.3cm
2005

我昨日之夢
A DREAM I DREAMED YESTERDAY
絹印、畫布
silkscreen on canvas
162x130.3cm
2006

等待春天的女人
WOMEN WAITING FOR SPRING
[TZW]
絹印、畫布
silkscreen on canvas
130.3x162cm
2005

擁擠之群
THE CROWD [TWXOZ]
絹印、畫布
silkscreen on canvas
162x130.3cm
2005

愛的終結
END OF LOVE
絹印、畫布
silkscreen on canvas
130.3x162cm
2006

午夜的女人
WOMEN IN THE MIDNIGHT
絹印、畫布
silkscreen on canvas
130.3x162cm
2005

永恆的愛
LOVE FOREVER [OPXTWE]
絹印、畫布
silkscreen on canvas
162x130.3cm
2005

初夏
EARLY SUMMER [TWPOX]
絹印、畫布
silkscreen on canvas
130.3x162cm
2006

花的禮讚
FLORAL TRIBUTE (TULIPS)
絹印、畫布
silkscreen on canvas
162x130.3cm
2006

走入原野
GOING OUT INTO THE FIELD
絹印、畫布
silkscreen on canvas
162x130.3cm
2006

春之兆
SIGNS OF SPRING [WQZY]
絹印、畫布
silkscreen on canvas
130.3x162cm
2007

女人的紐約
WOMEN'S NEW YORK [SSAAWA]
絹印、畫布
silkscreen on canvas
130.3x162cm
2007

我心中之旗
FLAG IN MY HEART [TXOZT]
絹印、畫布
silkscreen on canvas
162x130.3cm
2006

青春標竿
GUIDEPOST TO YOUTH
[HOTWOX]
絹印、畫布
silkscreen on canvas
130.3x162cm
2007

早晨醒來
WAKING UP IN THE MORNING
[TQSTW]
絹印、畫布
silkscreen on canvas
130.3x162cm
2007

花開紐約
FLOWERING NEW YORK [OPRT]
絹印、畫布
silkscreen on canvas
162x130.3cm
2005

萌芽
SPROUTING [TOXZS]
絹印、畫布
silkscreen on canvas
130.3x162cm
2006

我喜歡自己
I LIKE MYSELF [TOWHSQ]
絹印、畫布
silkscreen on canvas
130.3x162cm
2006

初春之兆
SIGNS OF EARLY SPRING [T.A.A.Z]
絹印、畫布
silkscreen on canvas
130.3x162cm
2005

波浪
WAVES [TWXZO]
絹印、畫布
silkscreen on canvas
130.3x162cm
2007

天國入口
ENTRANCE TO HEAVEN [TQWFV]
絹印、畫布
silkscreen on canvas
130.3x162cm
2007

女人的一生
WOMAN'S LIFE [T.WXO]
絹印、畫布
silkscreen on canvas
130.3x162cm
2005

宇宙之旅
JOURNEY TO THE UNIVERSE
[TZQMN]
絹印、畫布
silkscreen on canvas
130.3x162cm
2007

無限宇宙
INFINITY-COSMOS [TOWEY]
絹印、畫布
silkscreen on canvas
162x130.3cm
2007

星辰棲居之所
DWELLING OF STARS [TWXSS]
絹印、畫布
silkscreen on canvas
162x130.3cm
2007

青春時光
DAYS OF YOUTH [YOZMTO]
絹印、畫布
silkscreen on canvas
130.3x162cm
2007

生、老、病、死
BIRTH, AGING, SICKNESS AND
DEATH [QXPAT]
絹印、畫布
silkscreen on canvas
130.3x162cm
2007

晨之華
MORNING SPLENDOR [TWHIOW]
絹印、畫布
silkscreen on canvas
130.3x162cm
2007

無限的網與點
INFINITY NETS & DOTS

無限雙點
INFINITY DOUBLE DOTS
壓克力、畫布
acrylic on canvas
145.5x112cm
2013

無限的網
INFINITY NETS [AWPFE]
壓克力、畫布
acrylic on canvas
227.3x181.8cm
2013

藍色的網
BLUE NETS [WOSNE]
壓克力、畫布
acrylic on canvas
162x130.3cm
2012

無限的網
INFINITY DOTS [AHPRUS]
壓克力、畫布
acrylic on canvas
145.5x145.5cm
2012

無限的網
INFINITY NETS [SHOMC]
壓克力、畫布
acrylic on canvas
227.3x181.8cm
2013

無限的網
INFINITY NETS [ASWQH]
壓克力、畫布
acrylic on canvas
130.3x130.3cm
2011

雲
THE CLOUDS [PSSOW]
壓克力、畫布
acrylic on canvas
130.3x130.3cm
2008

無限的網
INFINITY NETS [TWHOQ]
壓克力、畫布
acrylic on canvas
3 panels:each 194x130.3cm
2006

無限的網
INFINITY-NETS [LPDWQ]
壓克力、畫布
acrylic on canvas
194x194cm
2013

無限的網
INFINITY NETS [QTAB]
壓克力、畫布
acrylic on canvas
145.5x145.5cm
2012

無限的網
INFINITY NETS [OOXSAN]
壓克力、畫布
acrylic on canvas
3 panels:each 145.5x112cm
2008

無限的網
INFINITY NETS [PADWH]
壓克力、畫布
acrylic on canvas
130.3x162cm
2011

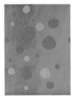

星之消融
OBLITERATION OF STARS
(COPPER)
壓克力、畫布
acrylic on canvas
259x194cm
2010

輪迴
TRANSMIGRATION
壓克力、畫布
acrylic on canvas
4 panels:each 194x130.3cm
2011

圓點執念
DOTS OBSESSION [FOPMU]
壓克力、畫布
acrylic on canvas
194x194cm
2013

紅點
RED DOTS [TVRS]
壓克力、畫布
acrylic on canvas
194x194cm
2013

圓點
DOTS [ABCDEF]
壓克力、畫布
acrylic on canvas
97x130.3cm
2008

無限的網
INFINITY-NETS[ZAALO]
壓克力、畫布
acrylic on canvas
162x162cm
2013

10歲左右 開始以圓點及網狀作為繪畫元素，利用水彩、粉彩、油彩繪製奇幻風格的畫作。

1957年 赴美後發表巨幅平面作品、軟雕塑以及使用鏡面、燈飾的環境雕塑作品。

1960年 後期進行大量偶發藝術活動，如人體彩繪、時尚秀、反戰 活動等。

1966年 參加第33屆威尼斯雙年展，發表作品〈自戀庭院〉並開始嘗試運用媒體的表現手法，如製作電影、發行報紙等。

1968年 自導自演的電影《消滅自己》獲得比利時第4屆國際短片獎、安娜堡電影節銀獎、第2屆馬里蘭電影節獎。於歐洲各國舉辦展覽及進行偶發藝術活動。

1973年 返日持續創作發表藝術作品，並發行多部小説及詩集。

1983年 小説作品《克里斯多夫男娼窟》獲得第10屆野性時代新人獎。

1986年 於法國加萊藝術博物館及多爾博物館舉辦個展。

1989年 於紐約國際藝術中心、英國牛津現代藝術博物館舉辦個展。

1993年 參加第45屆威尼斯雙年展。

1994年 開始創作戶外雕塑。於福岡健康中心、福岡美術館、直島文化村、霧島藝術之森、松本市美術館、日本新潟松代車站前、法國TGV里爾車站前、比佛利花園公園（比佛利山莊）、韓國安養市和平公園設置戶外雕塑，並於里斯本地鐵走道製作壁畫。

1996年後 以紐約畫廊為主要活動據點，榮獲國際美術評論家聯盟最佳作品獎1995/96及最佳作品獎1996/97。

1998年~1999年 於洛杉磯州立美術館舉辦大型回顧展，之後陸續巡迴至紐約現代美術館、沃克藝術中心、東京都現代美術館。

2000年 榮獲第50屆藝術選獎文部大臣獎、外務大臣獎。同年於法國當代藝術中心舉辦個展，之後陸續巡迴至巴黎日本文化會館、丹麥奧登斯美術館、法國土魯斯亞巴托當代藝術美術館、維也納藝術館、韓國首爾ARTSONJE藝術中心、韓國慶州ARTSONJE美術館。

2001年 榮獲朝日獎。

2002年 於松本市美術館舉辦開館紀念個展。

2003年 榮獲法國藝術及文學勳章、長野縣知事藝術文化功勞獎。

2004年 於森美術館舉辦個展《KUSAMATRIX》，參觀人次達52萬人。同年於東京國立近代美術館舉辦個展，之後陸續巡迴至京都國立近代美術館、廣島市現代美術館、熊本市現代美術館、松本市美術館。

2006年 榮獲藝術領域終生成就獎、旭日小綬獎、第18屆高松宮殿下紀念世界文化獎（繪畫領域）。

2008年 紀錄片《草間彌生 我最喜歡的我》上映。回顧展於荷蘭博曼斯美術館開始巡迴。受封為松本市名譽市民。

2009年 回顧展於雪梨近代美術館、紐西蘭威靈頓城市美術館開始巡迴。於紐約高古軒畫廊、比佛利山莊高古軒畫廊、倫敦維多利亞米羅藝廊、米蘭當代藝術展覽館等地舉辦個展。獲選為傑出文化功勞者。

2010年 於十和田市現代美術館舉辦個展。於同城市藝術廣場設置永久雕塑裝置藝術。參加雪梨雙年展、愛知三年展。於倫敦維多利亞米羅藝廊、巴黎當代藝術博覽會舉辦個展。

2011年 於羅馬高古軒畫廊、倫敦維多利亞米羅藝廊舉辦個展。歐美回顧展首站於馬德里索菲亞王后國家藝術中心博物館開幕，之後巡迴至巴黎龐畢度中心。於東京和多利美術館舉辦個展。秋季時參加中國成都雙年展，於布里斯本昆士蘭美術館舉辦個展。

2012年 於大阪國立國際美術館舉辦新作品個展，之後陸續巡迴至埼玉縣立美術館、松本市美術館、新潟市美術館。於倫敦泰特現代藝術館、紐約惠特尼美術館舉辦歐美回顧展。於倫敦維多利亞米羅藝廊舉辦個展。受封為新宿區榮譽區民。美國藝術暨文學學會會員。與路易威登合作〈LOUIS VUITTON × YAYOI KUSAMA Collection〉系列。

2013年~2015年 中南美巡迴回顧展於布宜諾斯艾利斯拉美藝術博物館揭開序幕，另於韓國大邱美術館開始亞洲巡迴個展。

年表

10歳の頃より水玉と網模様をモチーフに絵を描き始め、水彩、パステル、油彩などを使った幻想的な絵画を制作。

1957年渡米、巨大な平面作品、ソフトスカルプチャー、鏡や電飾を使った環境彫刻を発表する。1960年代後半にはボディ・ペインティング、ファッション・ショー、反戦運動など多数のハプニングを行う。1966年第33回ベニス・ビエンナーレに参加し、「ナルシスの庭」を発表。また映画製作や新聞の発行などメディアを使った表現にも着手。1968年自作自演の映画「草間の自己消滅」は第4回ベルギー国際短編映画祭に入賞、アン・アーバー映画祭で銀賞、第2回メリーランド映画祭にて受賞。ヨーロッパ各国でも展覧会、ハプニングを行う。

1973年帰国、美術作品の制作発表を続けながら、小説、詩集も多数発表。1983年小説「クリストファー男娼窟」で第10回野性時代新人賞を受賞。

1986年フランスのカレー市美術館、ドール美術館にて個展。1989年ニューヨーク国際芸術センター、イギリスオックスフォード美術館にて個展。1993年第45回ベニス・ビレに参加。

1994年より野外彫刻を手がける。福岡健康センター、福岡美術館、ベネッセ・アイランド直島文化村、霧島アートの森、松本市美術館、松代駅前（新潟）、TGV リール駅前（フランス）、ビバリー・ガーデンズ・パーク（ビバリーヒルズ）、平和公園（安養市、韓国）に野外彫刻を、リスボンの地下鉄通路に壁画を制作。

1996年からは主にニューヨークのギャラリーを中心に活動を始め、国際美術評論家連盟よりベストギャラリー賞1995/96、ベストギャラリー賞1996/97を受ける。

1998年から1999年にかけてロスアンゼルス・カウンティ・ミュージアムを皮切りに大回顧展がニューヨーク近代美術館、ウォーカーアートセンター、東京都現代美術館を巡回。

2000年　第50回芸術選奨文部大臣賞、外務大臣表彰を受賞。同年、フランス、コンソルシウムで始まった個展は、パリ日本文化会館、オーデンセ美術館（デンマーク）、レザバトア美術館（トゥールーズ）、クンストハーレーウイーン、アートソンジュ・センター（ソウル）、アートソンジュ・ミュージアム（慶州）を巡回。

2001年　朝日賞受賞。

2002年　松本市美術館開館記念個展。

2003年　フランス芸術文化勲章オフィシェ受勲、長野県知事表彰（芸術文化功労）受賞。

2004年　森美術館個展「クサマトリックス」（森美術館）は52万人を動員。同年、東京国立近代美術館より始まった個展が京都国立近代美術館、広島市現代美術館、熊本市現代美術館、松本市美術館を巡回。

2006年　ライフタイム　アチーブメント賞（芸術部門）、旭日小綬賞、高松宮殿下記念世界文化賞（第18回）絵画部門受賞 。

2008年　ドキュメンタリー映画「草間彌生　わたし大好き」公開。ボイマンス・ファン・ベーニンゲン博物館（オランダ）にて回顧展の巡回が始まる。松本市名誉市民に推挙される。

2009年　シドニー現代美術館、ウェリントンシティギャラリー（ニュージーランド）回顧展巡回。ガゴシアン・ニューヨーク、ガゴシアン・ビバリーヒルズ、ヴィクトリア・ミロギャラリー（ロンドン）、Padiglione d'Arte Contemporanea（ミラノ）の各都市で個展。文化功労者に選出される。

2010年　十和田市現代美術館にて個展、同市アート広場に恒久彫刻インスタレーションを展示。シドニービエンナーレ、あいちトリエンナーレに参加。ヴィクトリア・ミロギャラリー（ロンドン）、Fiac（パリ）で個展。

2011年　ガゴシアンギャラリー（ローマ）、ヴィクトリア・ミロギャラリー（ロンドン）で個展。国立ソフィア王妃芸術センター（マドリッド）から欧米回顧展がスタート、ポンピドゥー・センター（パリ）へ巡回。ワタリウム美術館（東京）個展。秋には成都ビエンナーレ（中国）参加、クイーンズランド・アートギャラリー（ブリスベン）で個展。

2012年　国立国際美術館（大阪）で新作個展が巡回開始、その後埼玉県立美術館、松本市美術館、新潟市美術館へ巡回。欧米回顧展がテート・モダン（ロンドン）、ホイットニー美術館（ニューヨーク）へ巡回。ヴィクトリア・ミロギャラリー（ロンドン）で個展。新宿区栄誉区民顕彰。アメリカン・アカデミー・オブ・アーツ＆レターズ会員。ルイ・ヴィトンとのコラボレーション「LOUIS VUITTON × YAYOI KUSAMA Collection」を発表。

2013年-2015年　中南米巡回回顧展がラテンアメリカアート美術館（ブエノスアイレス）より、またアジア巡回個展がテグ美術館（韓国）より開始。

BIOGRAPHY

Yayoi Kusama

Born in Nagano Prefecture.
Avant-garde artist, novelist.

Started to paint using polka dots and nets as motifs at around age ten ,and created fantastic paintings in watercolors, pastels and oils.

Went to the United States in 1957. Showed large paintings, soft sculptures, and environmental sculptures using mirrors and electric lights.

In the latter 1960s, staged many happenings such as body painting festivals, fashion shows and anti-war demonstrations. Launched media-related activities such as film production and newspaper publication.

In 1968, the film "Kusama's Self-Obliteration"which Kusama produced and starred in won a prize at the Fourth International Experimental Film Competition in Belgium and the Second Maryland Film Festival and the second prize at the Ann Arbor Film Festival. Held exhibitions and staged happenings also in various countries in Europe.

Returned to Japan in 1973. While continuing to produce and show art works, Kusama issued a number of novels and anthologies.

In 1983, the novel "The Hustlers Grotto of Christopher Street" won the Tenth Literary Award for New Writers from the monthly magazine Yasei Jidai.

In 1986, held solo exhibitions at the Musee Municipal, Dole and the Musee des Beaux-Arts de Calais, France.

In 1989, solo exhibitions at the Center for International Contemporary Arts, New York and the Museum of Modern Art, Oxford, England.

In 1993, participated in the 45th Venice Biennale.

Began to create open-air sculptures in 1994. Produced open-air pieces for the Fukuoka Kenko Center, the Fukuoka Municipal Museum of Art, the Bunka-mura on Benesse Island of Naoshima, Kirishima Open-Air Museum and Matsumoto City Museum of Art, in front of Matsudai

Station, Niigata,TGV's Lille-Europe Station in France, Beverly Gardens Park, Beverly hills, Pyeonghwa Park, Anyang and a mural for the hallway at subway station in Lisbon.

Began to show works mainly at galleries in New York in 1996. A solo show held in New York in the same year won the Best Gallery Show in 1995/96 and the Best Gallery Show in 1996/97 from the International Association of Art Critics in 1996.

From1998 to 1999, a major retrospective of Kusama's works which opened at the Los Angeles County Museum of Art traveled to the Museum of Modern Art, New York, the Walker Art Center and the Museum of Contemporary Art, Tokyo.

In 2000, Kusama won The Education Minister's Art Encouragement Prize and Foreign-Minister's Commendations. Her solo exhibition that started at Le Consortium in France in the same year traveled to Maison de la culture du Japon, Paris, KUNSTHALLEN BRANDTS ÆDEFABRIK, Denmark, Les Abattoirs, Toulouse, KUNSTHALLE Wien, Art Sonje Center, Seoul.

Received the Asahi Prize in 2001.

Solo exhibition hold in Matsumoto City Museum Of Art in 2002.
The French Ordre des Arts et des Lettres (Officier), and the Nagano Governor Prize (for the contribution in encouragement of art and culture) in 2003

In 2004, Her solo exhibition "KUSAMATRIX" started at Mori Museum in Tokyo. This exhibition drew visitors totaling 520,000 people. In the same year,another solo exhibition started at The National Museum of Modern Art, Tokyo.

In 2005, it traveled to The National Museum of Modern

Art, Kyoto, Hiroshima City Museum of Contemporary Art, Contemporary Art Museum, Kumamoto, Matsumoto City Museum of Art.

Received the 2006 National Lifetime Achievement Awards, the Order of the Rising Sun, Gold Rays with Losette and The Praemium Imperiale -Painting- in 2006.

In 2008, Documentary film : "Yayoi Kusama, I adore myself" released in Japan and also screened at international film festival and museum.
Exhibition tour started at Museum Boijmans Van Beuningen in Rotterdam, traveled to Museum of Contemporary Art Sydney in Australia in 2009, City Gallery Wellington in New Zealand. Conferred the honorary citizen of Matsumoto city.

Solo exhibition at Gagosian Gallery NY and LA, Victora Miro Gallery in London and Padiglione d'Arte Contemporanea in Milan. Honored as Person of Cultural Merits in Japan in 2009.

In 2010, solo exhibition and permanent outdoor sculpture at Towada Art Center in Japan.Participated in Sydney Biennale and Aichi Triennale. Solo exhibition at Victoria Miro Gallery in London.

2011, solo exhibition at Gagosian gallery (Roma), Victoria Miro gallery (London). Europe and North America retrospective tour started at Museo Nacional Centro De Arte Reina Sofia, Madrid and travelled to Centre Pompidou (Paris), TATE MODERN (London) and Whitney Museum (New York). Solo exhibition at Watari Art Museum (Tokyo). Participated in the 2011 Chengdu Biennale (China). Solo exhibition program at Queensland Art Gallery (Brisbane).

2012, "Eternity of Eternal Eternity", domestic solo exhibition tour started at National Museum of Art, Osaka and travelled The Museum of Modern Art, Saitama, Matsumoto City

Museum of Art, Matsumoto, Nigata City Art Museum, Nigata, Shizuoka Prefectural Museum, Shizuoka, Oita Art Museum, Oita, Japan. Shinjuku Honorary Citizen Award. The American Academy of Arts and Letters Foreign Honorary Membership. Collaborated with Louis Vuitton creative director Marc Jacobs for the collection "LOUIS VUITTON × YAYOI KUSAMA Collection".

2013-2015, Latin America retrospective tour "Yayoi Kusama, Obsesión infinita [Infinite Obsession]" started at Malba – Fundación Costantini(Buenos Aires) and traveled to Centro Cultural Banco do Brazil (Rio de Janeiro and Brasilia) and Instituto Tomie Ohtake(São Paulo), Museo Tamayo (Mexico City). "KUSAMA YAYOI, A Dream I Dreamed", an Asia touring exhibition of over 100 recent works opened at Daegu Art Museum (Korea), followed by the Museum of Contemporary Art Shanghai and Seoul Arts Center (Seoul), and will continue to other Asian venues through 2015.

KUSAMA YAYOI. A Dream I Dreamed
草間彌生
亞洲巡迴展台灣站

台中站圖錄

2015/6/6-2015/8/30
國立台灣美術館 101展覽室
週二至週五09:00-17:00；六日09:00-18:00

指導單位	文化部
主辦單位	國立臺灣美術館、KUSAMA Enterprise、旺旺中時媒體集團時藝多媒體、閣林文創股份有限公司
發 行 人	黃才郎、蔡紹中
總 策 畫	黃才郎、林宜標、楊培中
策 展 人	金善姬
助理策展	黃瀅潔
撰 文	陸蓉之

策展團隊
國立臺灣美術館　陳昭榮、蔡昭儀、林明賢、王婉如、薛燕玲、林晉仲、郭芳杏、梁伯忠、黃麗華
　　　　　　　　劉木鎮、劉忠毅、何宗游
時藝多媒體　　　黃瀅潔、向銳穎、王若憶、楊惠鈞、黃子亮、陳韻如、潘淑文、游雨璇、黃振修
　　　　　　　　吳詩萍、林芳代、謝志祥、蕭安秀
閣林文創　　　　楊培達、陳佩貞、林　彤、呂惠鈞、姚翊慧、蔡馥米、李宜方、江育綺、王琳雅

企畫編輯	黃瀅潔、向銳穎、王若憶
設計製作	林守襄
文稿翻譯	黃詩蘋、Kate Lim、飯田玲子、碧詠國際翻譯社、Glen Lucas
圖版授權	Copyright of Yayoi Kusama, Courtesy of Ota Fine Arts, Tokyo / Singapore, Victoria Miro, London, David Zwirner, New York, KUSAMA Enterprise
出 版 者	時藝多媒體傳播股份有限公司
	台北市艋舺大道303號
	TEL：02-6630-3888
	FAX：02-6632-9123
	Website：www.mediasphere.com.tw
出版日期	中華民國104年6月6日
定 價	新台幣1000元
I S B N	978-986-88377-8-2

KUSAMA YAYOI . A Dream I Dreamed

Catalogue of Taichung

2015/6/6-2015/8/30
Gallery 101, National Taiwan Museum of Fine Arts

Organized by: National Taiwan Museum of Fine Arts, KUSAMA Enterprise,
                      Media Sphere Communication Ltd., Want Want China Times Media Group and Greenland Creative Co., Ltd.
Publishers: Tsai-Lang Huang, Shao-Chung Tsai
Directors: Tsai-Lang Huang, Bill Lin, Pei-Chung Yang
Curator: Kim Sunhee, Director of Daegu Art Museum
Assistant Curator: Justine Huang
Author: Victoria Lu

Exhibition organizers:

National Taiwan Museum of Fine Arts:
          Chao-Jung Chen, Chao-Yi Tsai, Ming-Hsien Lin, Wan-Ju Wang, Yen-ling Hsueh, Chin-Chung Lin, Fang-Shing Kuo
          Bor-Jong Liang, Li-Hua Huang, Mu-Chun Liu, Chung-Yi Liu, Thung-yu Ho
Media Sphere Communications Ltd.:
          Justine Huang, Jui-Ying Hsiang, Jo-I Wang, Hui-Chun Yang, Sherlock Huang, Yun-Ju Chen, Jocelyn Pan, Carrie Yu
          Stan Huang, Wallis Wu, Yoshiyo Lin, Chih-Hsiang Hsieh, Annie Hsiao
Greenland Creative Co., Ltd.:
          Pei-Da Yang, Pei-Chen Chen, Tung Lin, Hui-Chun Lu, Yi-Huei Yao, Fu-Mi Tsai, Yi-Fang Lee, Yu-Chi Chiang, Lin-Ya Wang

Chinese editing: Justine Huang, Jui-Ying Hsiang, Jo-I Wang,
Catalogue design: Tess Lin
Translation and editing: Amber Huang, Kate Lim, Reiko Iida, Albion Proworks, Glen Lucas

Copyright Credit: Copyright of Yayoi Kusama, Courtesy of Ota Fine Arts, Tokyo /
                        Singapore, Victoria Miro, London, David Zwirner, New York, KUSAMA Enterprise

Publisher: Media Sphere Communications Ltd.
                        ADD: 303 Banka Blvd., F6, Wanhua Dist., Taipei City 10855, Taiwan, R.O.C
                        TEL: 886-2-6630-3888
                        FAX: 886-2-6632-9123
                        Website: www.mediasphere.com.tw
Publishing Date: 6th June 2015
Price: NTD$1,000